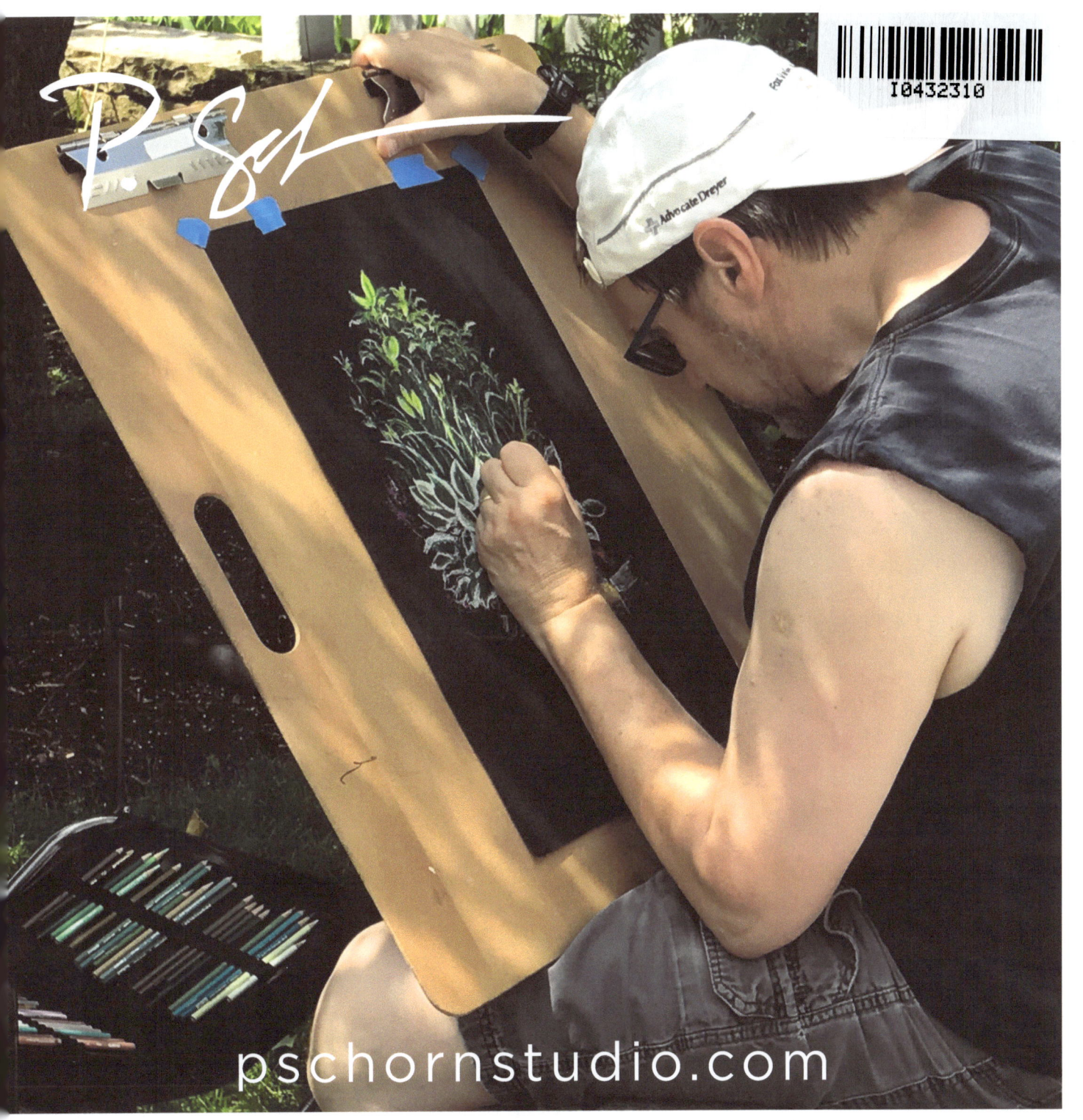
pschornstudio.com

Life is in the Details Vol. II

Life is in the Details was published at a time when I was a few months into being cancer free. I decided *why not* share what I have been doing the last several years.

With what I went thru with the cancer (how unexpected it was) the timing was great, because you never know when everything may be taken away from you.

The first book consisted of many of the renderings that I did over the last several years. It did not contain how I did my art. I did supply a lot of tips, which are also in this book.
I'm filling in a lot of gaps that I missed the first time. More tips and insight into how I did the renderings.

This is a not a step-by-step instructional book, but more of a sharing of my ideas and process of my art which has been very successful.

As any artist knows not everything you do works out as expected, over the years I have ripped up many, many drawings that just did not work. I've learned a lot by trial and error.

Some of the images shown in the book are cropped to fit the page format. I tried to explain some of the main tips and process I used for the rendering. If you have a little experience with color pencil you will pick-up on how I did the drawings very quickly.

The pencils I use are the Prismacolor Premier Softcore, I really like them being wax based. Because I can get great blending effects, good details and easy to purchase.

I also at times add fine line pens, markers and an ebony pencil to get more details. Also have done pastels and watercolors with the color pencil to create other effects.

I have shared my story, images and tips with Voyage Chicago Magazine Oct 2017, Colored Pencil Magazine, as the featured artist; October 2016 and a special article August 2019.

Remember that there is as many ways to draw as there is artists drawing.
There is no one way to do a drawing. I'm just sharing some ways that I did mine.

Artist Statement

I am a color pencil artist that paints with the pencil

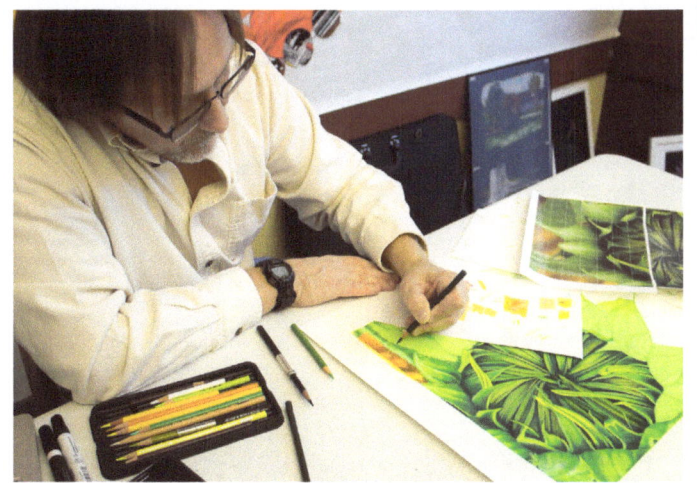

My botanical renderings are not drawings of plant specimens as seen in scientific books, rather, they are renderings of plants as seen through the eye of an artist. I can look at the ground and can see the shapes, light and shadows. I typically do not draw the entire location.

I focus on a portion of the scene and what makes that interesting. Whether that be the individual leaf, flower, or snapshot of the ground, I bring the details to life.

In my drawings, I focus on achieving realism and try to put in as much detail as possible. I want the viewer to look and then get lost in the scene as if they were standing in it.

Background

I attended Eastern Illinois University on an Art Scholarship, I graduated with a BA, double majoring in Graphic Design and 2D Studio Art. I have been an independent graphic artist for more than 30 years.

With much encouragement from my family, I started drawing in earnest several years ago. I have been featured in art publications and have done many solo & group exhibits, demos, and workshops.

I have received many awards at shows and several pieces in this book have already been sold.

pschornstudio.com

All copyrights and reproduction rights are retained by Philip Schorn.
The artwork shown may not be reproduced without the express written consent of Philip Schorn.

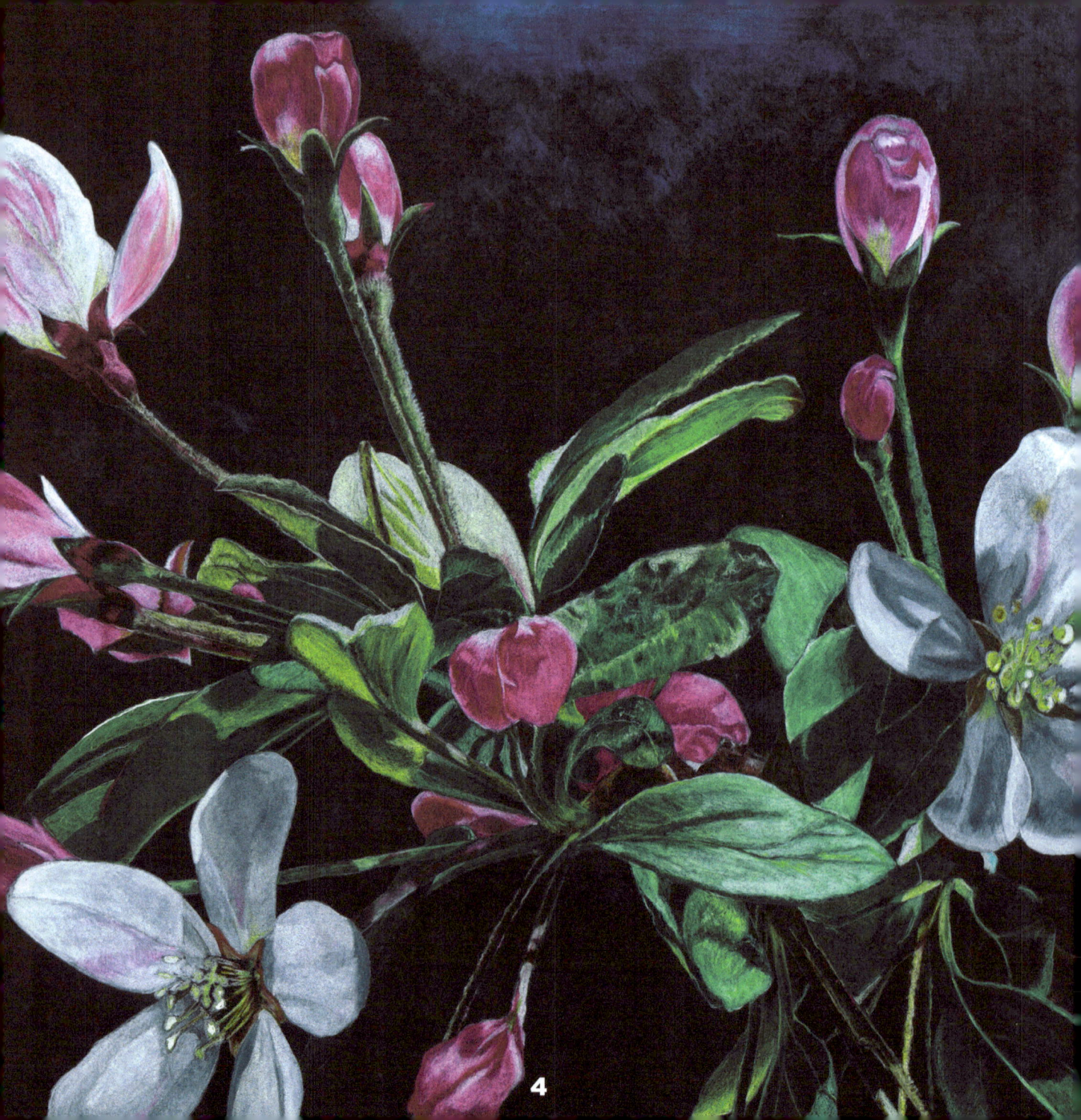

Title: Backyard Crabtree in Bloom

Size: 20" x 15"

Paper: 400 Series Black Artagain Paper

Insight:
- The whites were done by putting down a cool gray 20% and then white on top and then the red and other colors.
- The background was done with Prismacolor ArtStix, these are large chunks of color pencil without the wood.
- Then I used a OMS (odorless mineral spirits) and short angled No. 3 brush. It has stiff bristles that I use to mix and dissolve the pigment and wax to give that painterly look.
- I used a white pencil to blend my colors, it gives a creamy look, yellow, chartreuse and cream will do the same.
- The black paper is more toothy so your pencil get worn down faster and get more crumbs.

- **TIP:** Try not to use an eraser on black, it will scuff the paper and change the texture of where you erased.

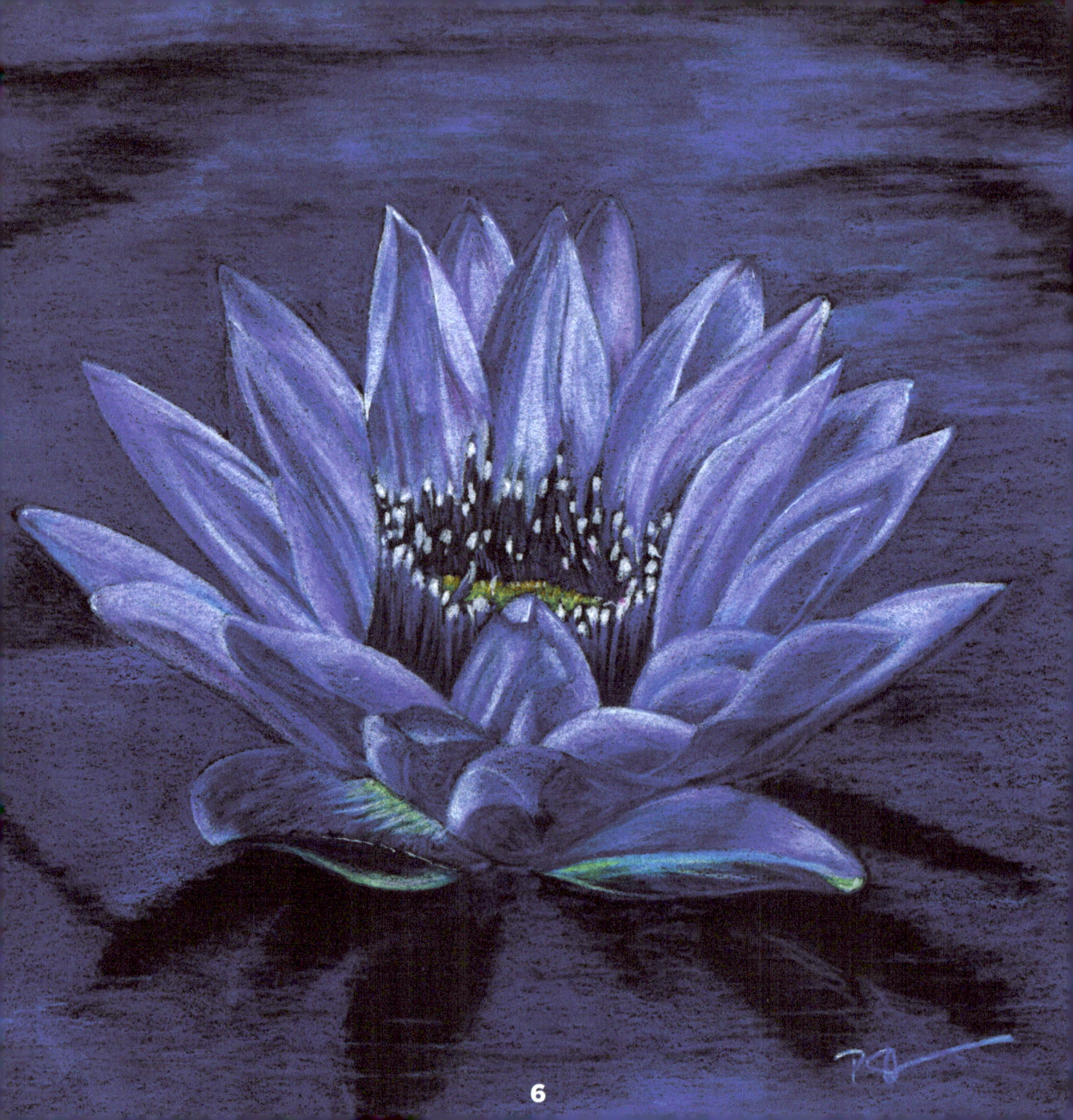

Title: Blue Water Lily

Size: 7" x 7"

Paper: Bee Black Bristol Board, (Bee is the manufacturer)

Insight:
- The background was done with Prismacolor® Art Stix and pencils. Then I used the OMS (odorless mineral spirits) to mix the colors.
- A white gel pen was used to add the white in the middle of the lily.
- The petals were done by laying down a violet blue and then white.
- White is an excellent blending color to add on top of other colors. If you add a color on top of the white, you loose ability to get a creamy look that is needed for the petals.

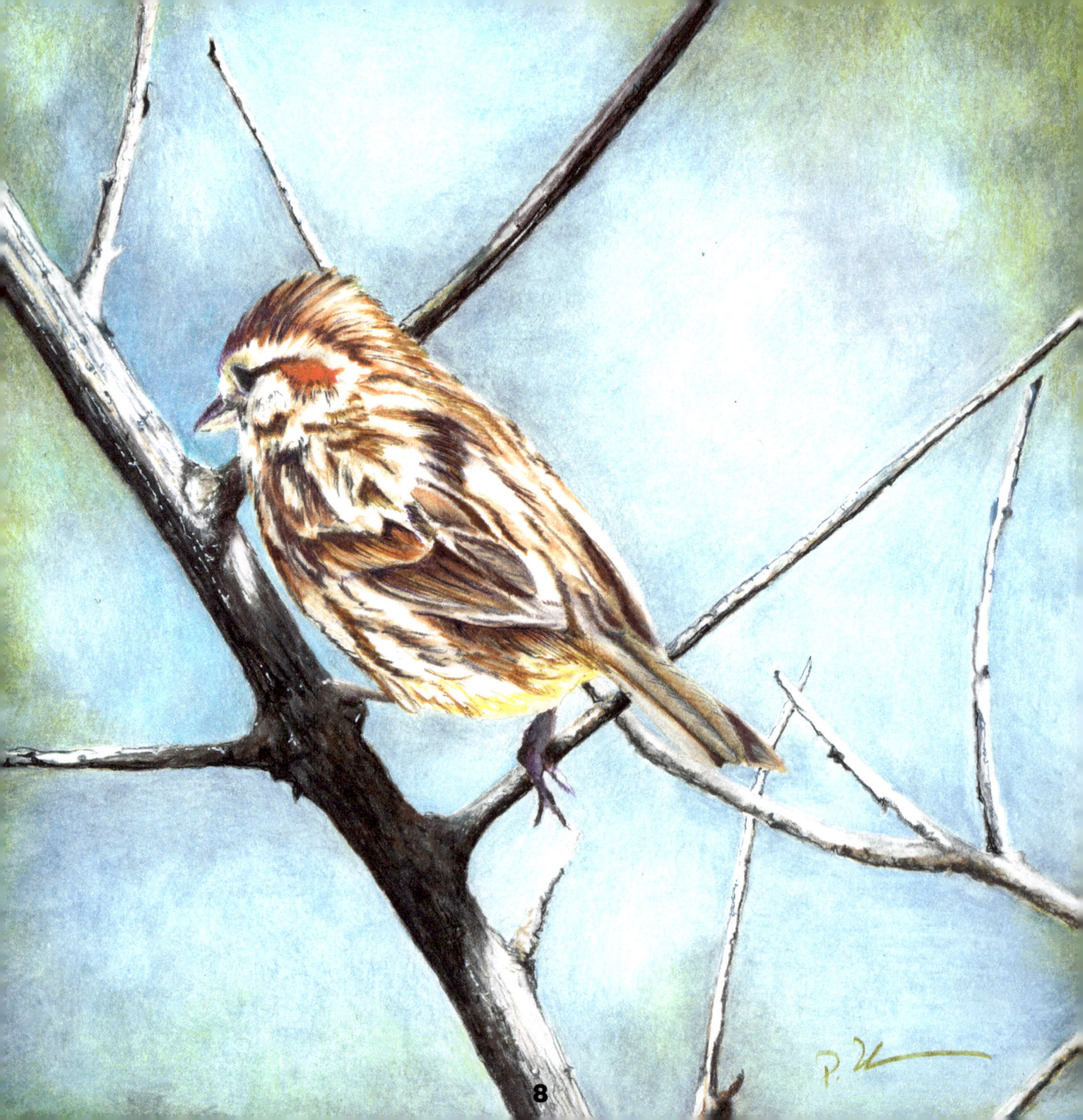

Title: House Finch

Size: 8" x 8"

Paper: Strathmore 400 Series Smooth Bristol

Insight:
- I started with the bird and then the branches.
- The background was done entirely with color pencils, drawing small strokes and overlapping them as I went along.
- I used a blending pen and OMS with a stiff bristle brush to dissolve my colors.

- **TIP:** Draw small, it let's you control the flow of the picture.
- I start with what I think is the hardest part to draw first.

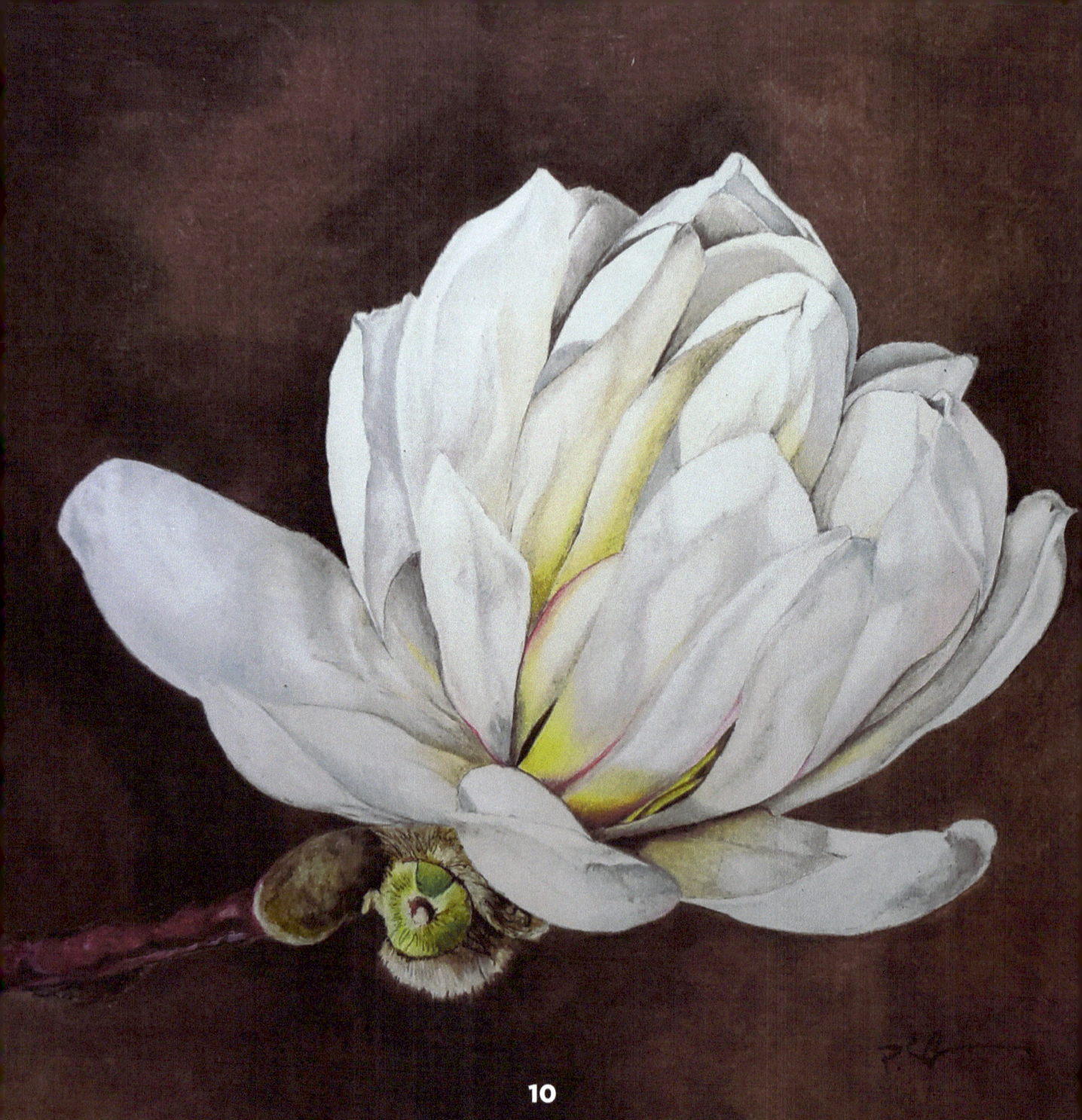

Title: Backyard Magnolia

Size: 8.5" x 8.5"

Paper: Strathmore 400 Series Smooth Bristol

Insight:
- I started with the petals, used a cool gray 10% and warm gray 10%. Then added white to blend the grays, then used a warm gray 50% for shadows, adding other colors needed.
- The background was done entirely with color pencils, drawing small strokes and overlapping them as I went along.
- I used a blending pen and OMS with a stiff bristle brush to dissolve my colors.

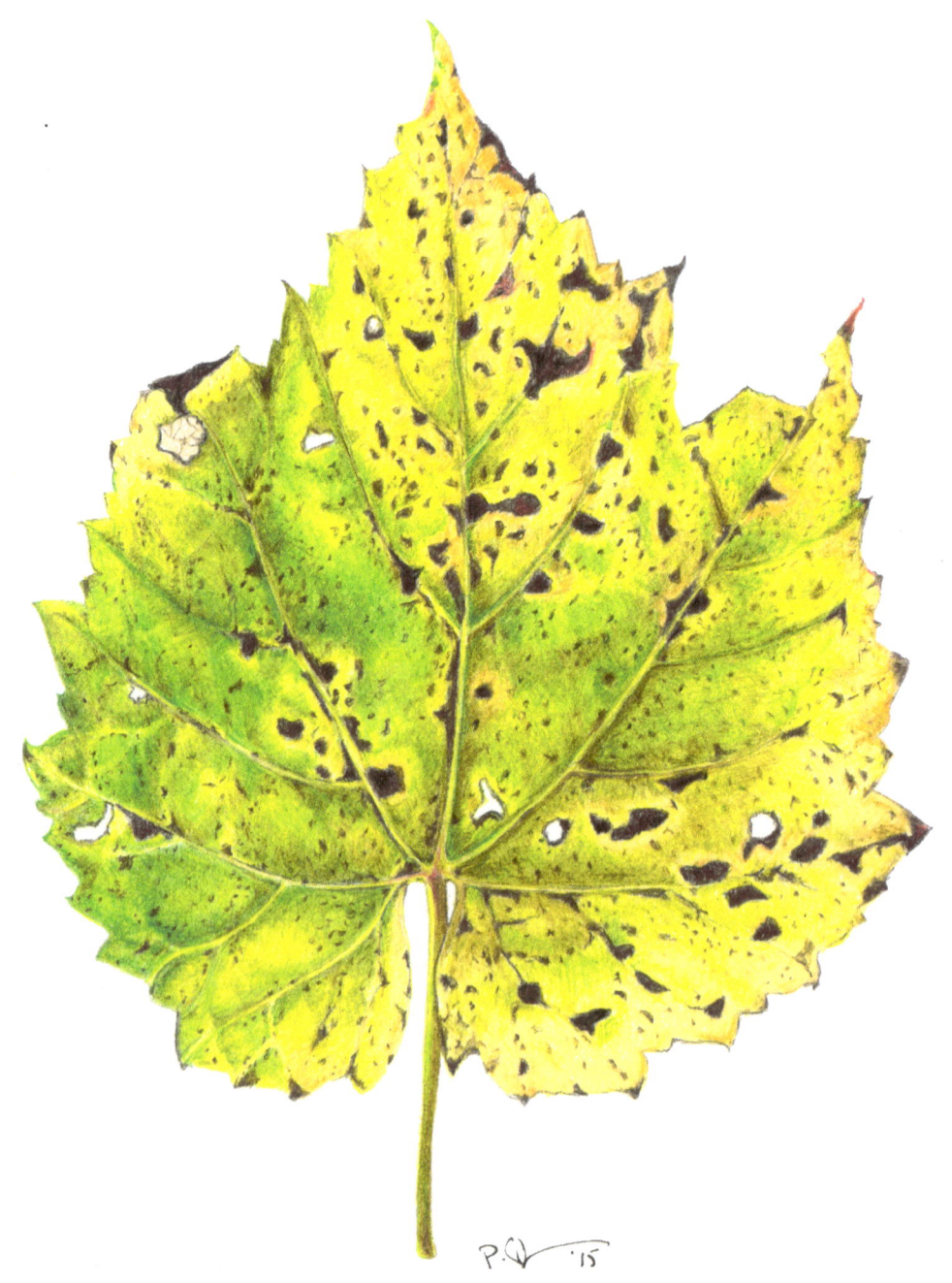

Title: Leaf No. 7

Size: 7" x 9"

Paper: Strathmore 300 Series Smooth Bristol

Insight:
- This image was one of my earlier renderings. This is 100% colored pencil.
- The image was one of many featured in the Oct. 2016 Color Pencil magazine.

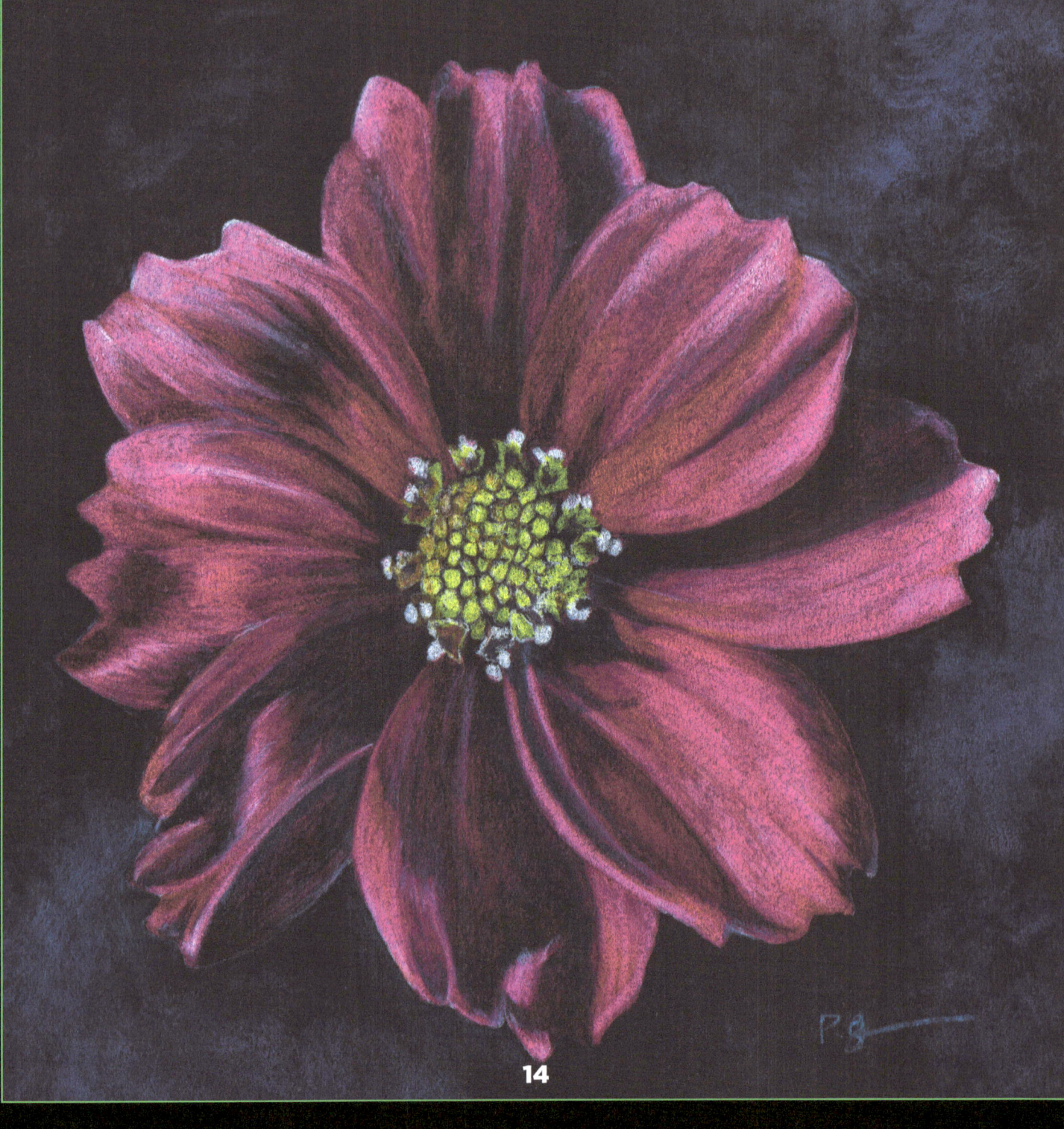

Title: Red Flower II

Size: 8.5" x 8.5"

Paper: Bee Black Bristol Board

Insight:
- I started with the flower, layering dark colors first, then adding white to make the highlights. By adding the white last, it gave the petals a more creamy look. The white pencil is a great blending color.
- The background was done with Indigo Blue, True Blue and Black pencils and Art Stix. Then I used a OMS wash to blend the colors.

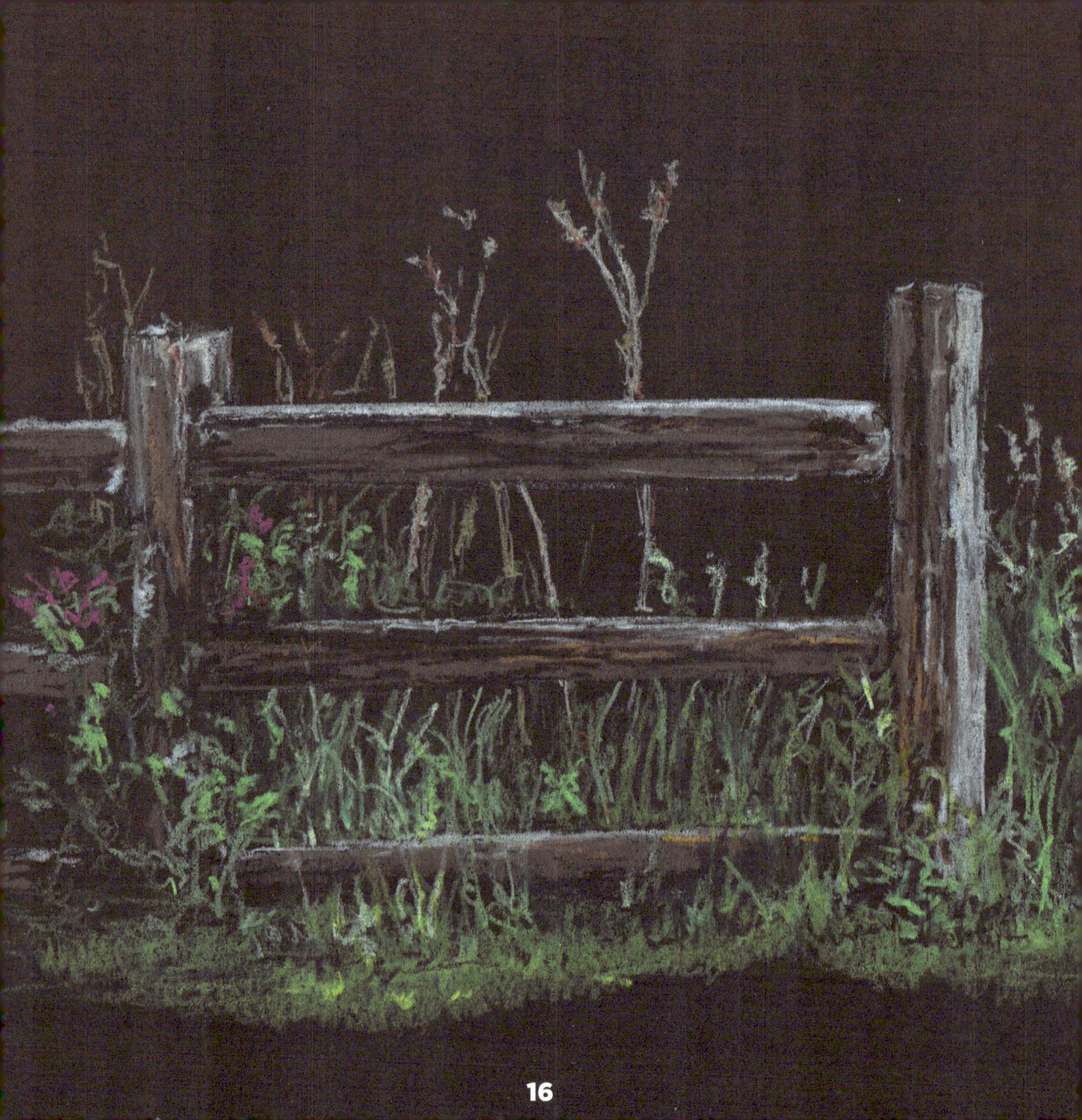

Title: Lakewood Fence

Size: 10" x 6"

Paper: Strathmore 400 Series Black Artagain

Insight:
- A plein-air drawing done at Lakewood Forest preserve.
- A more loose drawing style than what I normally do.

- **TIP:** Plein-air drawing is a good way to see and draw in a looser format. Colors are more vibrant than what you will get in a photograph.

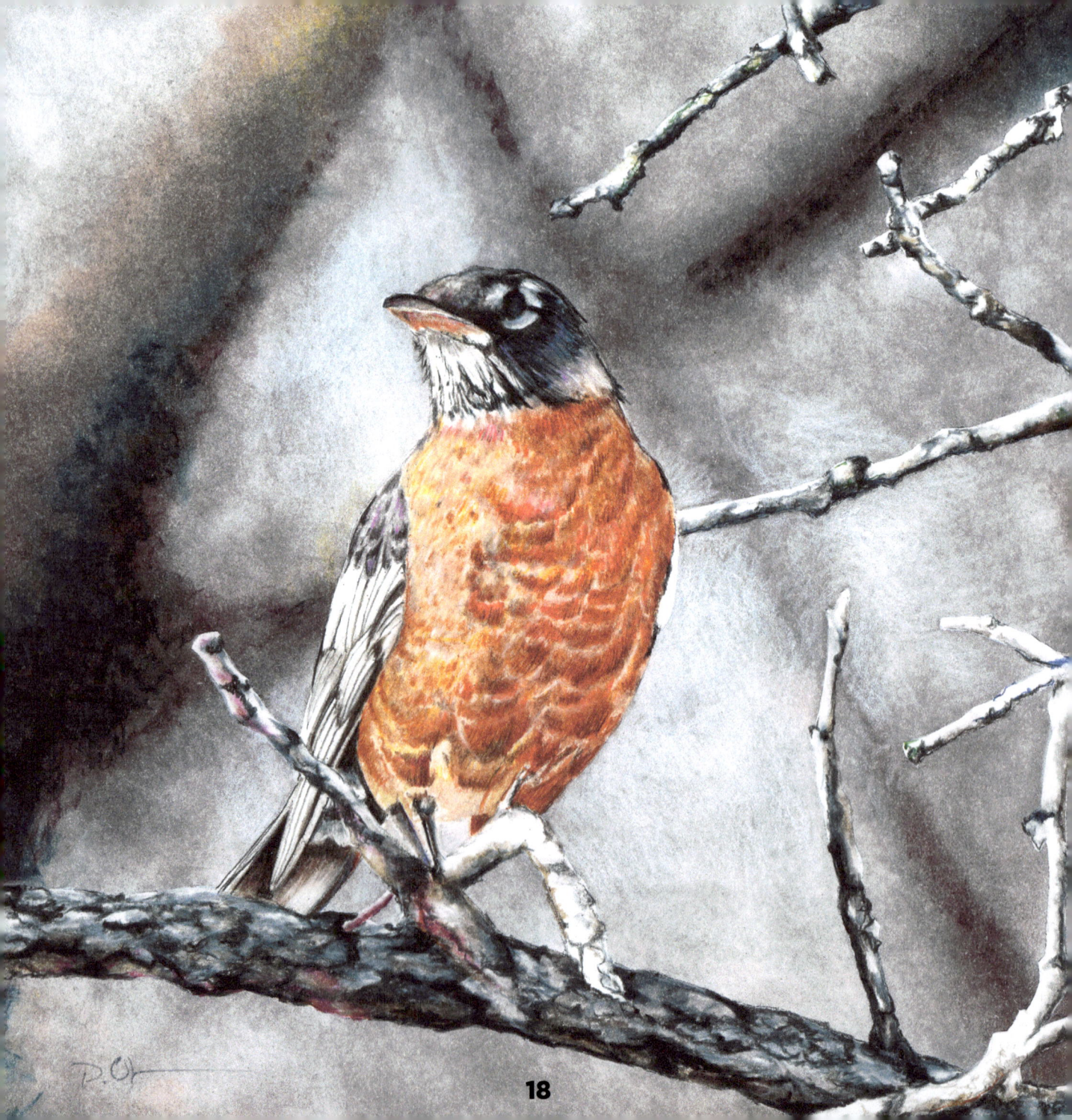

Title: American Robin

Size: 8" x 8"

Paper: Strathmore 400 Series White Smooth Bristol.

Insight:
- The background was done with pastels, the bird and branches was done with color pencil.
- I started by lightly penciling in the outline of the bird and branches. Then I covered the entire drawing with frisket.
- I then cut the frisket with a xacto knife only around the image.
- I pulled up the frisket to only expose the background to where I'm going to apply the pastels.
- After I did my background in pastel, I sprayed with a workable fixative. This was done so I can add more pastel if needed. Once I finished my pastels and spayed again. I lifted up the remainder of the frisket. This is the area where I used my color pencils.

- **TIP:** Remember to use a paper or acetate under your hand, you sill can smear the pastels if your not careful.

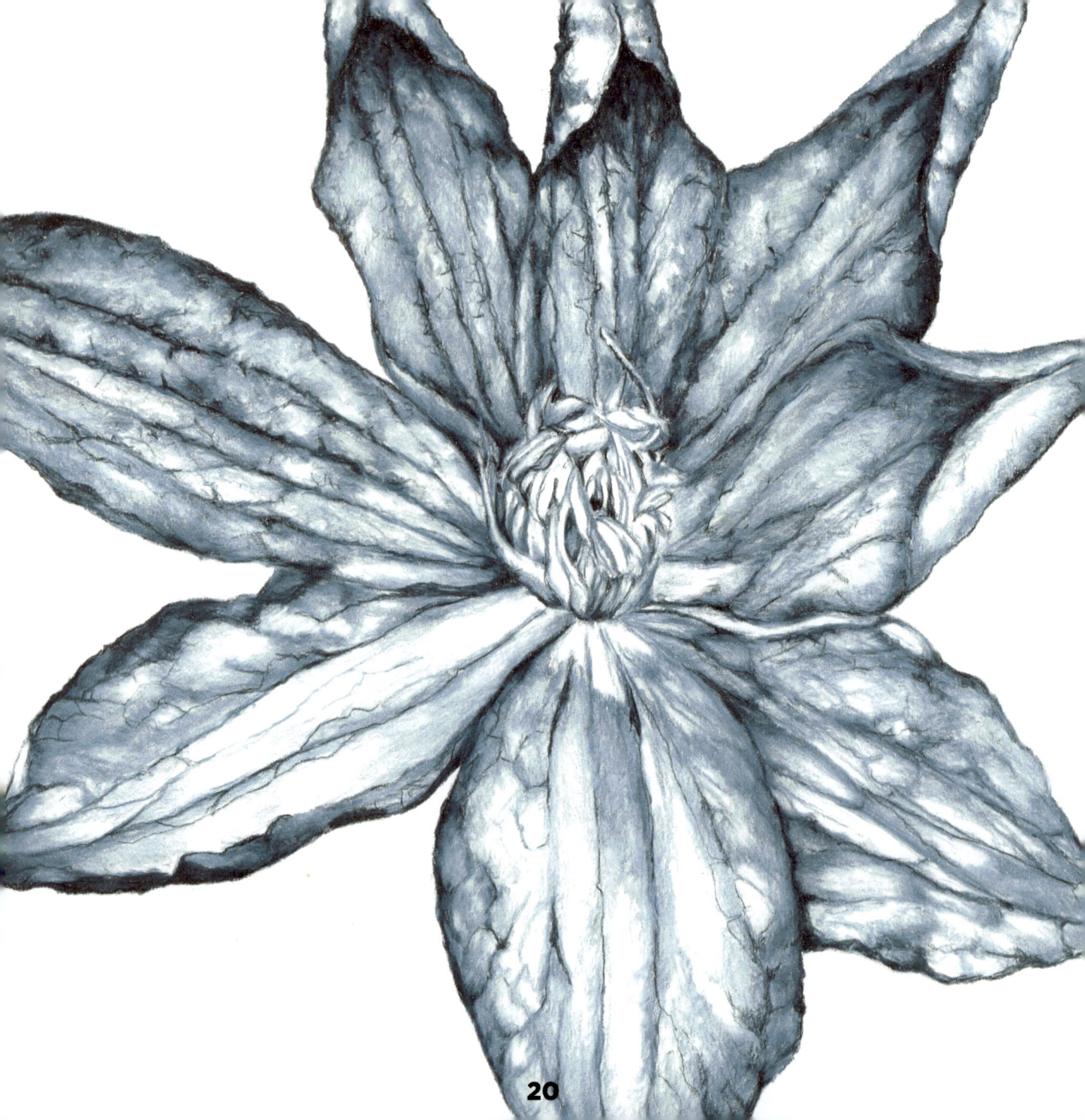

Title: Black & White Clematis

Size: 8" x 10"

Paper: Strathmore 400 Series White Smooth Bristol.

Insight:
- Only two color pencils used for this rendering. The white and black color pencil.
- I started by using only the black pencil as if it were a graphite pencil.
- Drawing the black lightly, because the black will darken up a few levels once you add white, make sure you test first.
- I added more black where needed and used more white to blend.
- I also used a blending pen to mix the white and black.

- **TIP:** This is a perfect example where white is an excellent blending color. It is much more waxer than most colors.

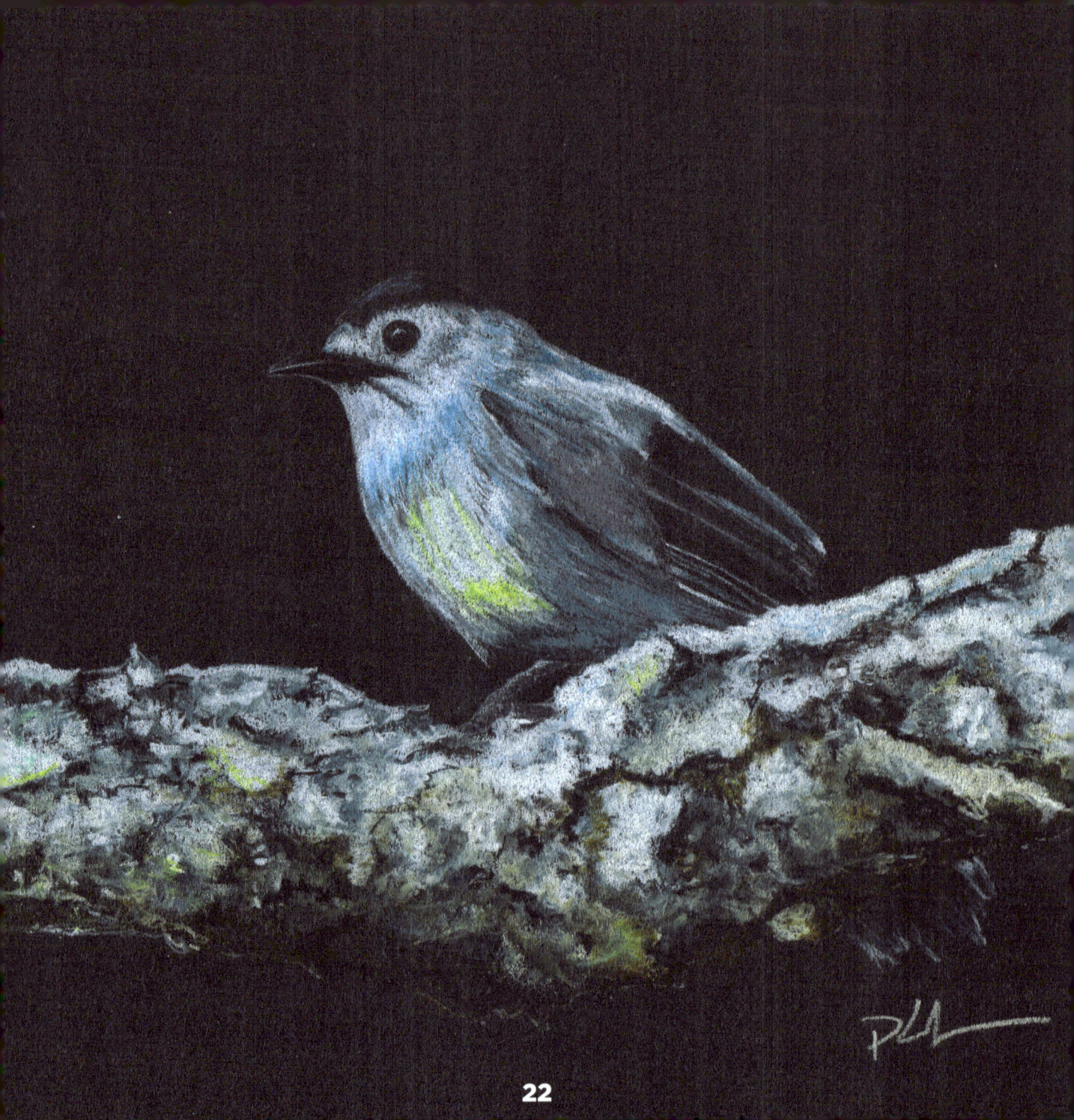

Title: Tree Swallow

Size: 8" x 8"

Paper: Bee Black Bristol Board.

Insight:
- No background was done
- I used white graphic paper to transfer my outline to the paper.
- 100% color pencil
- Make sure not to use an eraser on a area that are not going to put any color, it will scuff the paper.

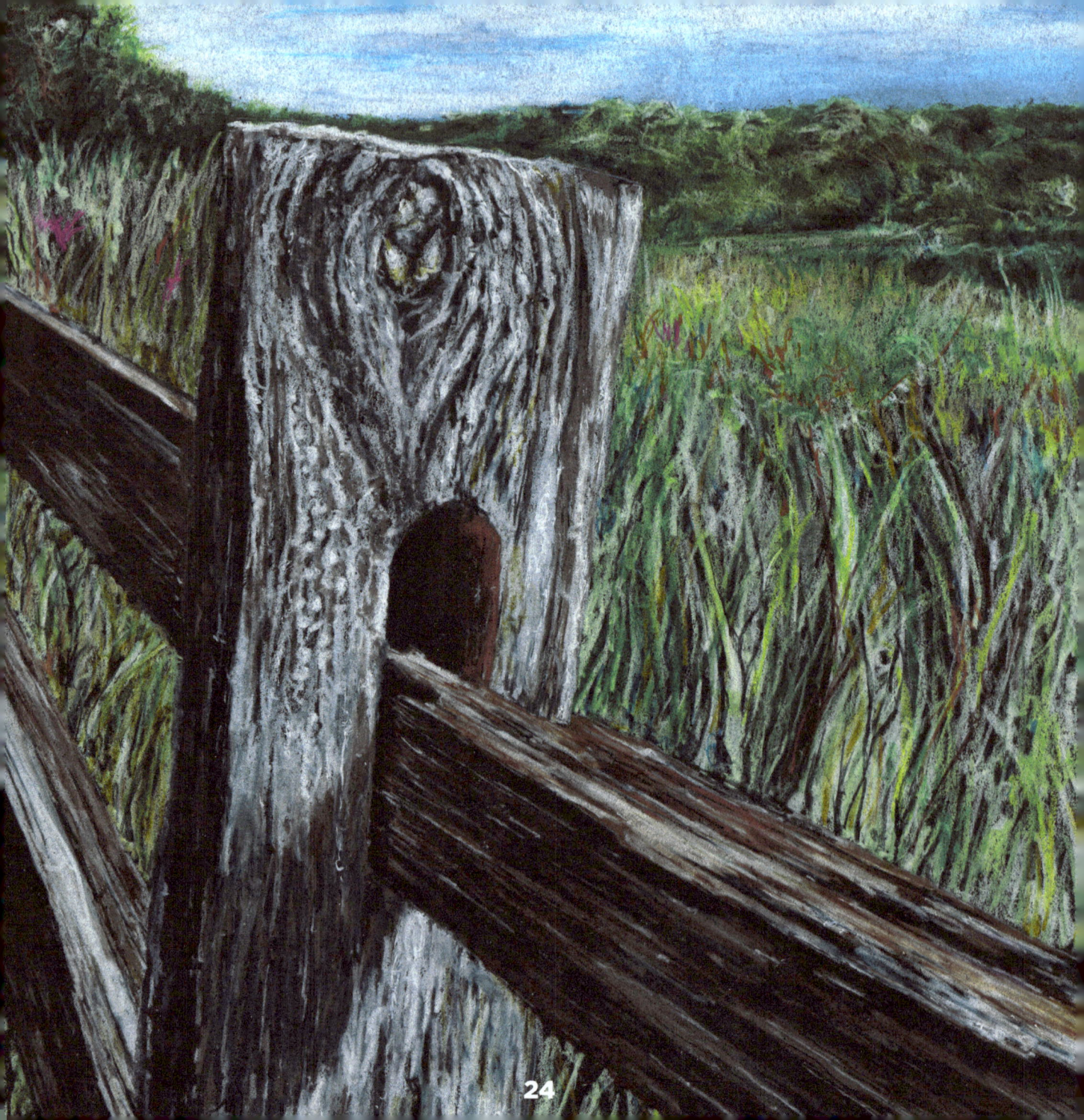

Title: Independence Grove Fence Post

Size: 8" x 12"

Paper: Strathmore 400 Series Black Artagain

Insight:
- 100% color pencil.
- For this subject and textures I wanted to achieve, the more toothy paper worked for me.

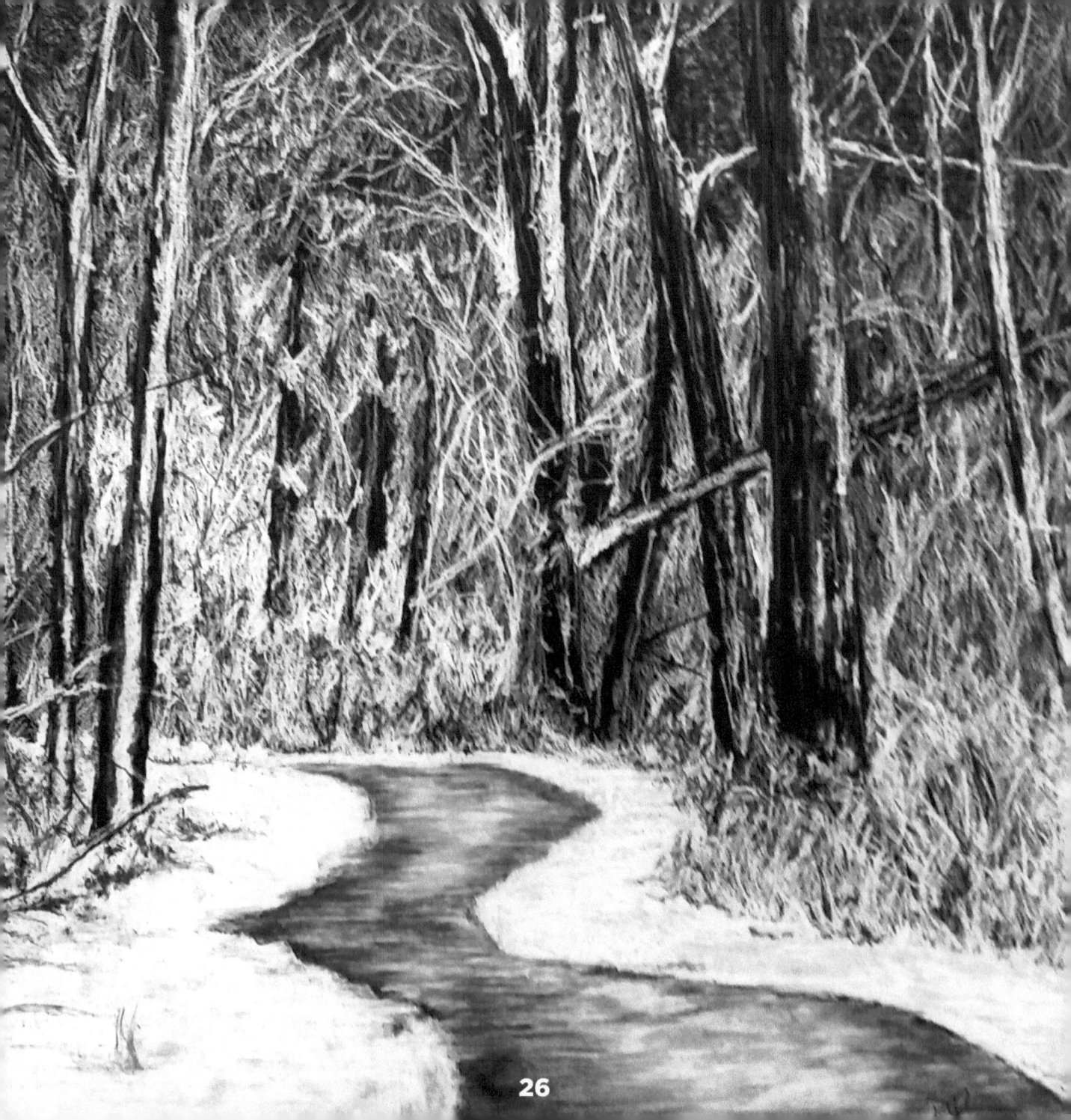

Title: Winter's Path

Size: 20" x 30"

Paper: Strathmore 400 Series Black Artagain

Insight:
- Used only the black and white color pencil and art stix.
- The art stix give you the ability to add more color, but in a more looser style.
- Only a small portion of the rendering is shown, I used the height of the trees to give more depth to the path.
- This path has been the source for several of my renderings.

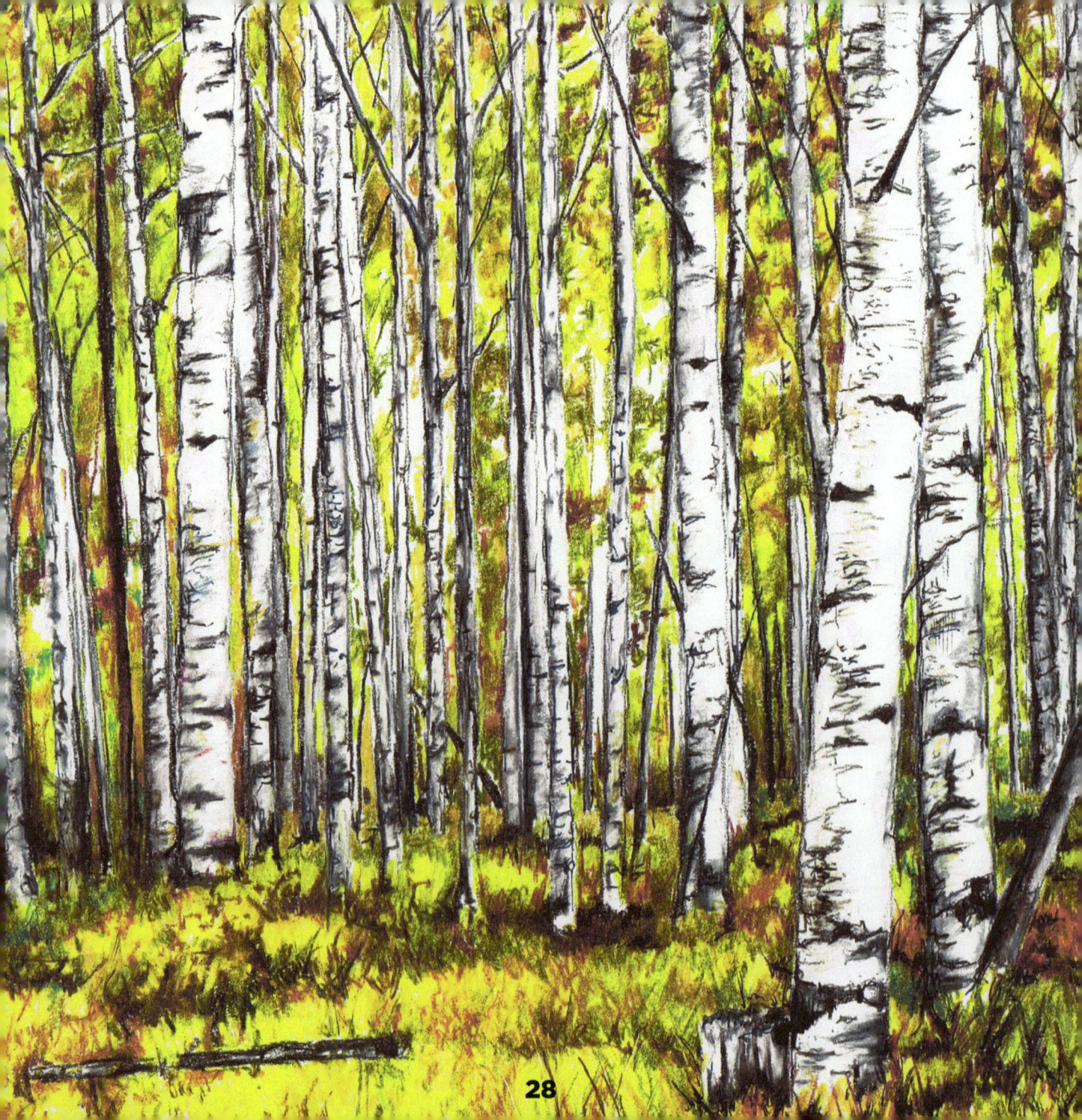

Title: Birch Forest

Size: 20" x 7"

Paper: Strathmore 400 Series White Smooth Bristol

Insight:
- I was really intrigued by the texture of the birches.
- A looser feel but with the detail I want.
- I used fine line pens to add details in the trees.

- **TIP:** If you use ink or paint on top of the color pencil, let it dry for a moment, because it will smear.

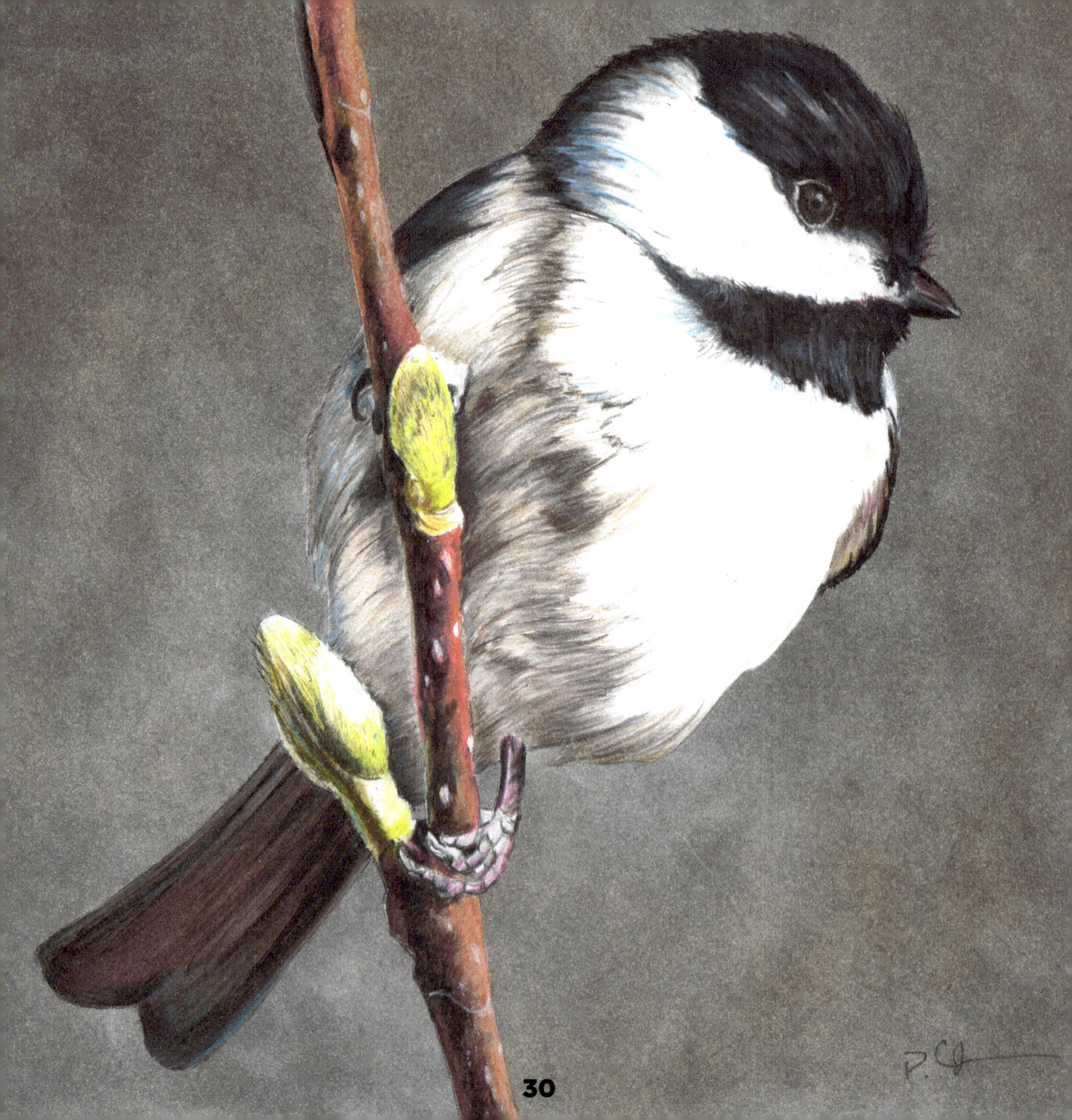

Title: Chickadee

Size: 8" x 8"

Paper: Strathmore 400 Series White Smooth Bristol.

Insight:
- The background was done with pan pastels, the bird and branches was done in color pencil.
- I started by lightly penciling in a outline of the bird and branches. Then I covered the entire drawing with frisket.
- I then cut the frisket with a xacto knife only around the image.
- I pulled up the frisket to only expose the background, this is where I'm going to use pastels.
- After I did my background in pastel, I sprayed with a workable fixative. This was done so I can add more pastel if needed.
- Once I finished my pastels and spayed. I lifted up the remainder of the frisket. This is the area where I used my color pencils.

- **TIP:** Pastels are dusty, be careful where you use them.

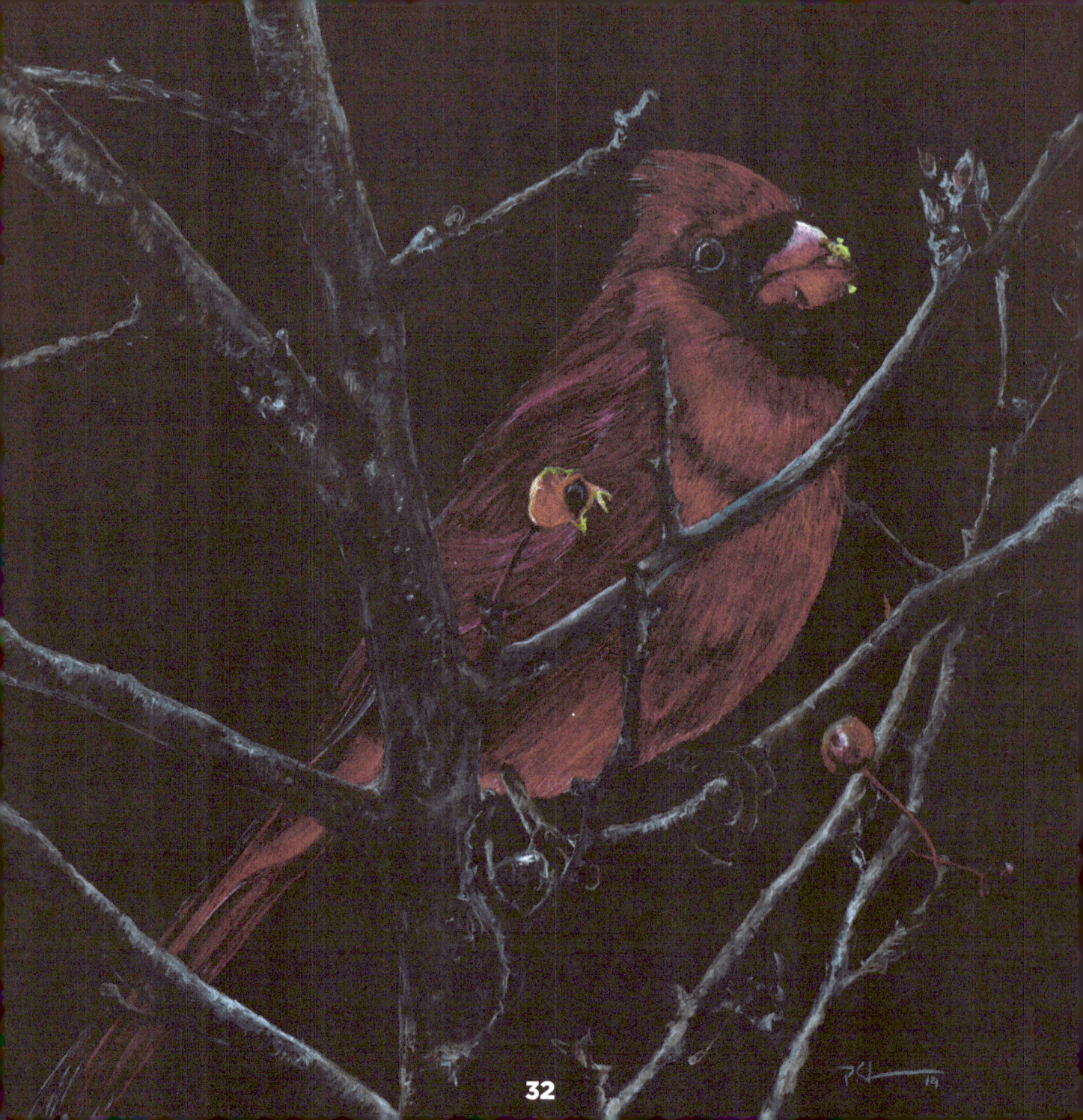

Title: Messy Cardinal

Size: 12" x 12"

Paper: Strathmore 400 Series Black Bristol.

Insight:
- No background was done.
- I used white graphic paper to transfer my outline to the paper.
- 100% color pencil.

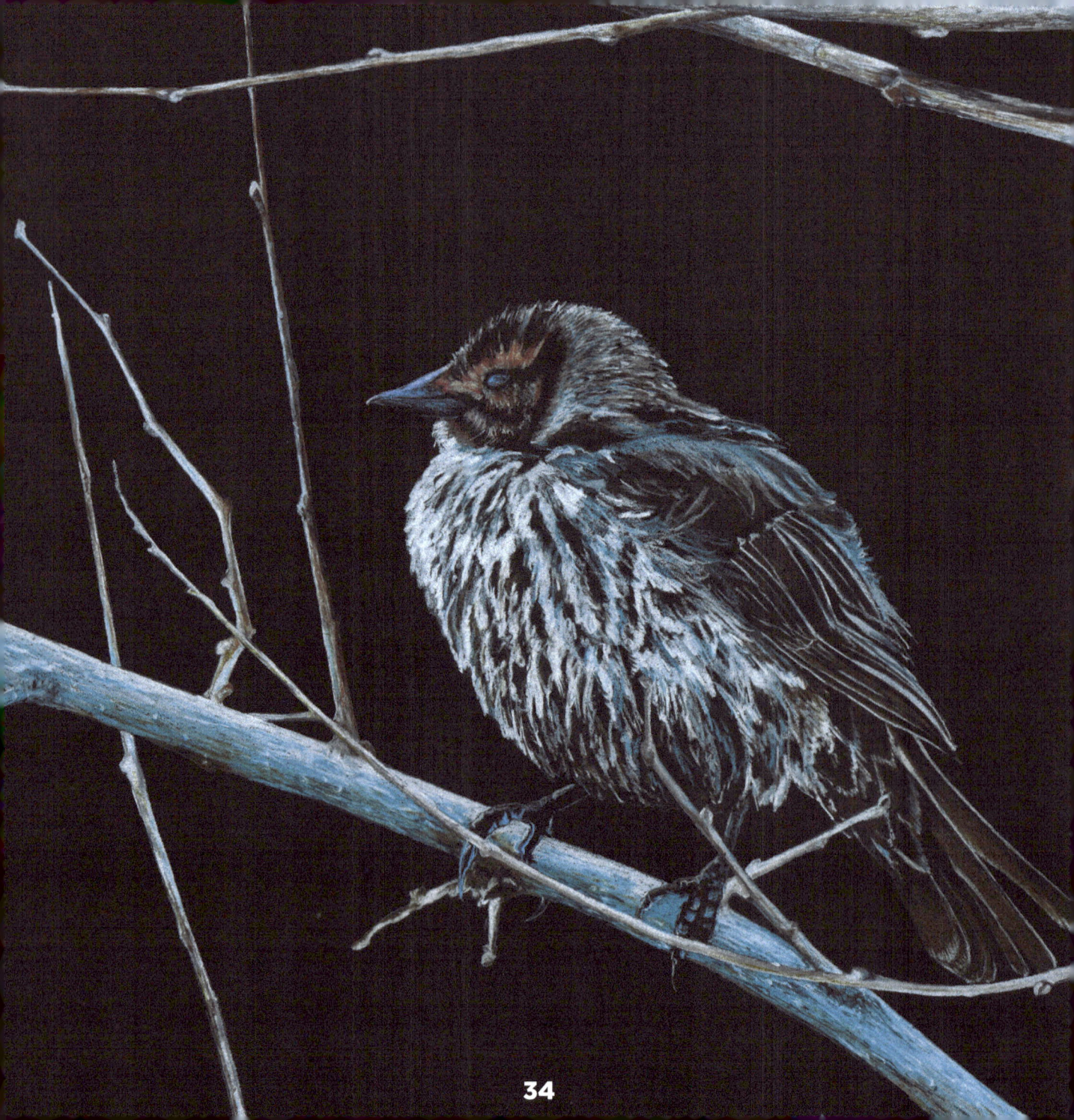

Title: Female Red Wing Black Bird

Size: 12" x 12"

Paper: Strathmore 400 Series Black Artagain

Insight:
- No background was done
- I used white graphic paper to transfer my outline to the paper.
- 100% color pencil
- I really was interested in the texture of the feathers, done by overlapping heavy strokes of color pencil.

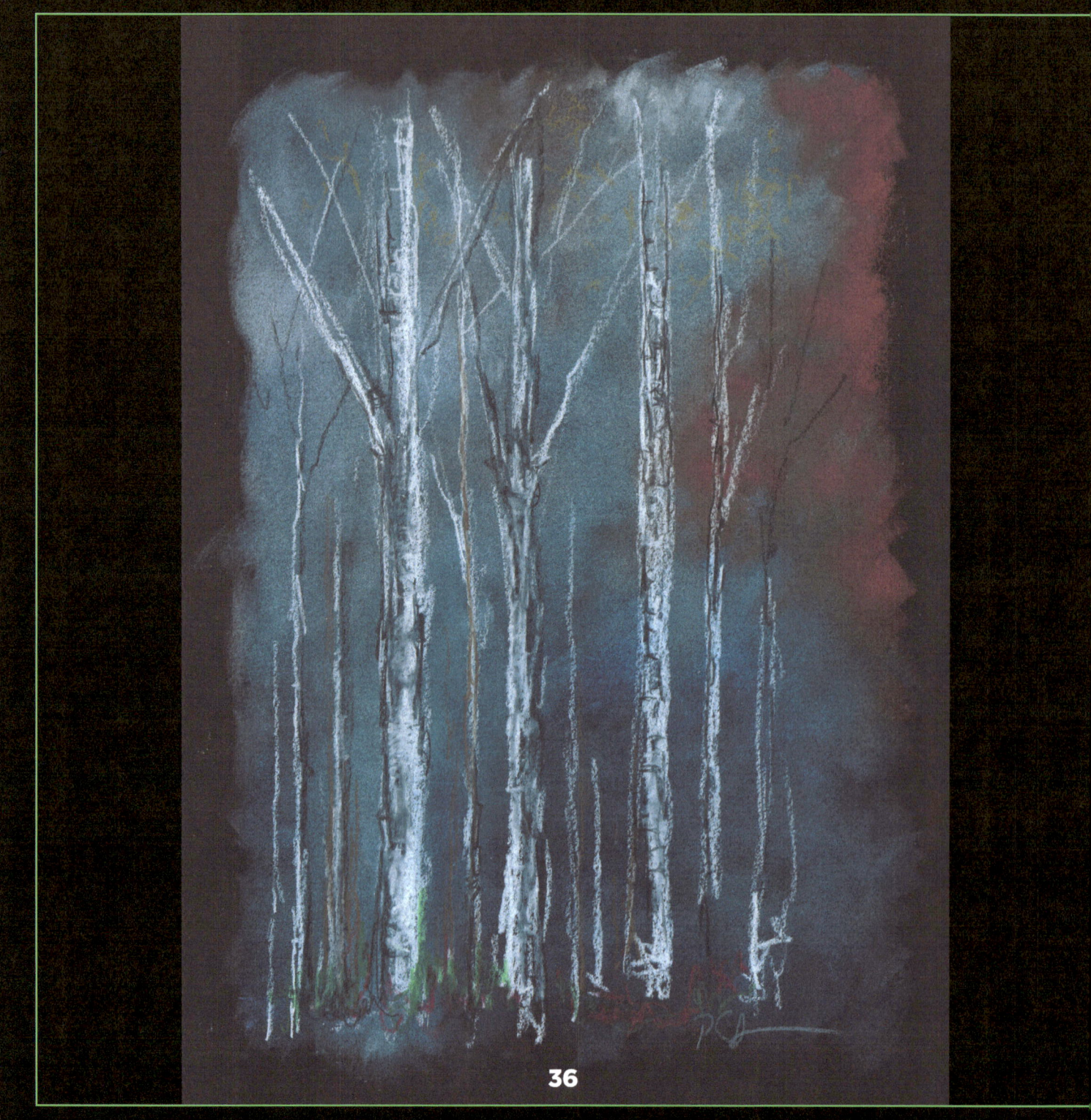

Title: Untitled

Size: 7" x 9"

Paper: Strathmore 400 Series Black Artagain

Insight:
- Pan Pastels were used for the background.
- Once I was done with the pastels, I sprayed with a workable fixative, then used the color pencils on top.
- Once all the drawing is done, I sprayed with a gloss final finish, it adds more depth to the colors.

- **TIP:** Pan Pastels are great to work with, but they can smear like the sticks do.

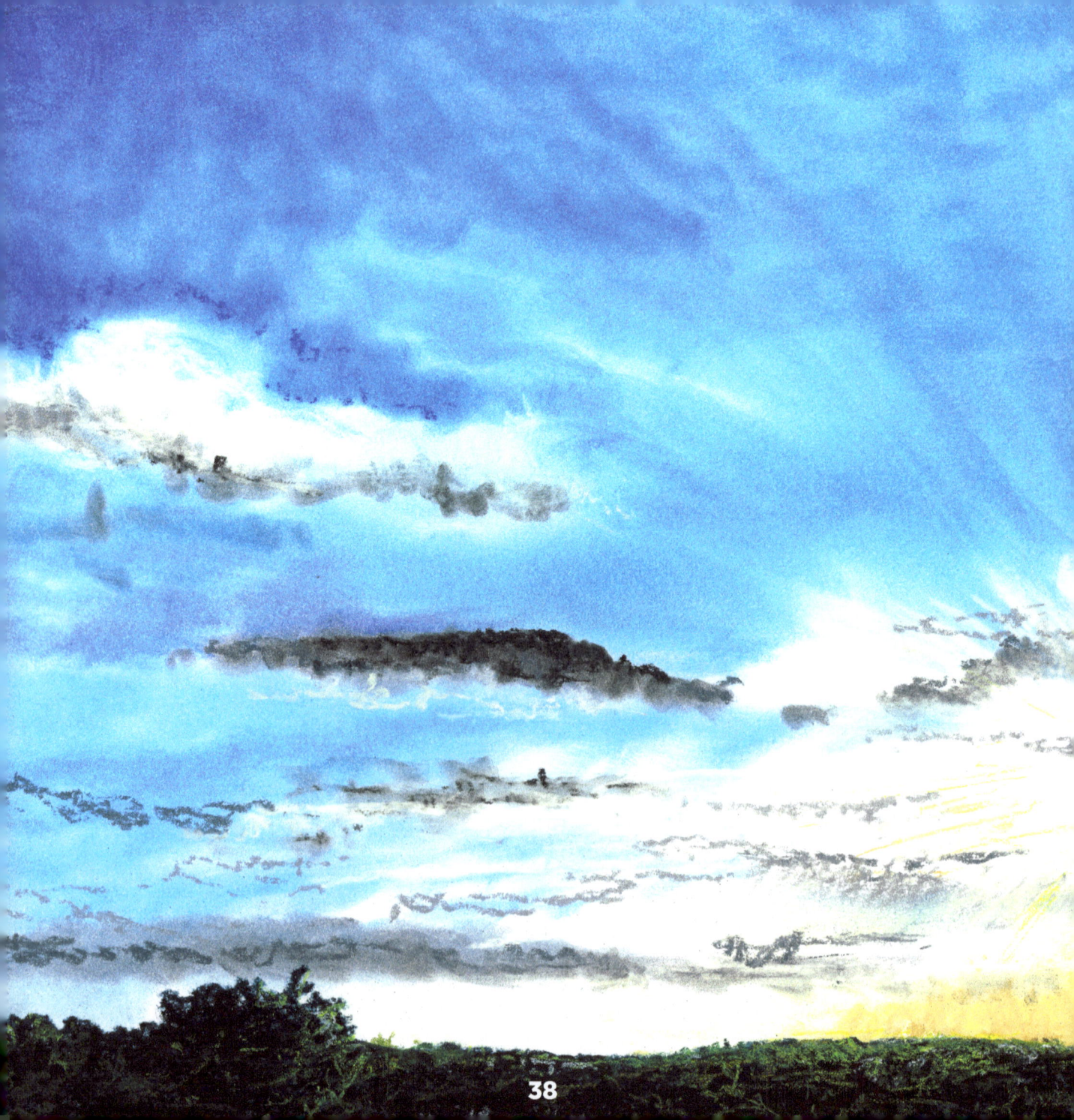

Title: Kansas Sunset

Size: 20" x 10"

Paper: Strathmore 400 Series White Vellum Board.

Insight:
- Pan Pastels and Stick Pastels were used for the background.
- Once I was done with the pastels, I sprayed with a workable fixative, then used the color pencils on top for details and highlights.

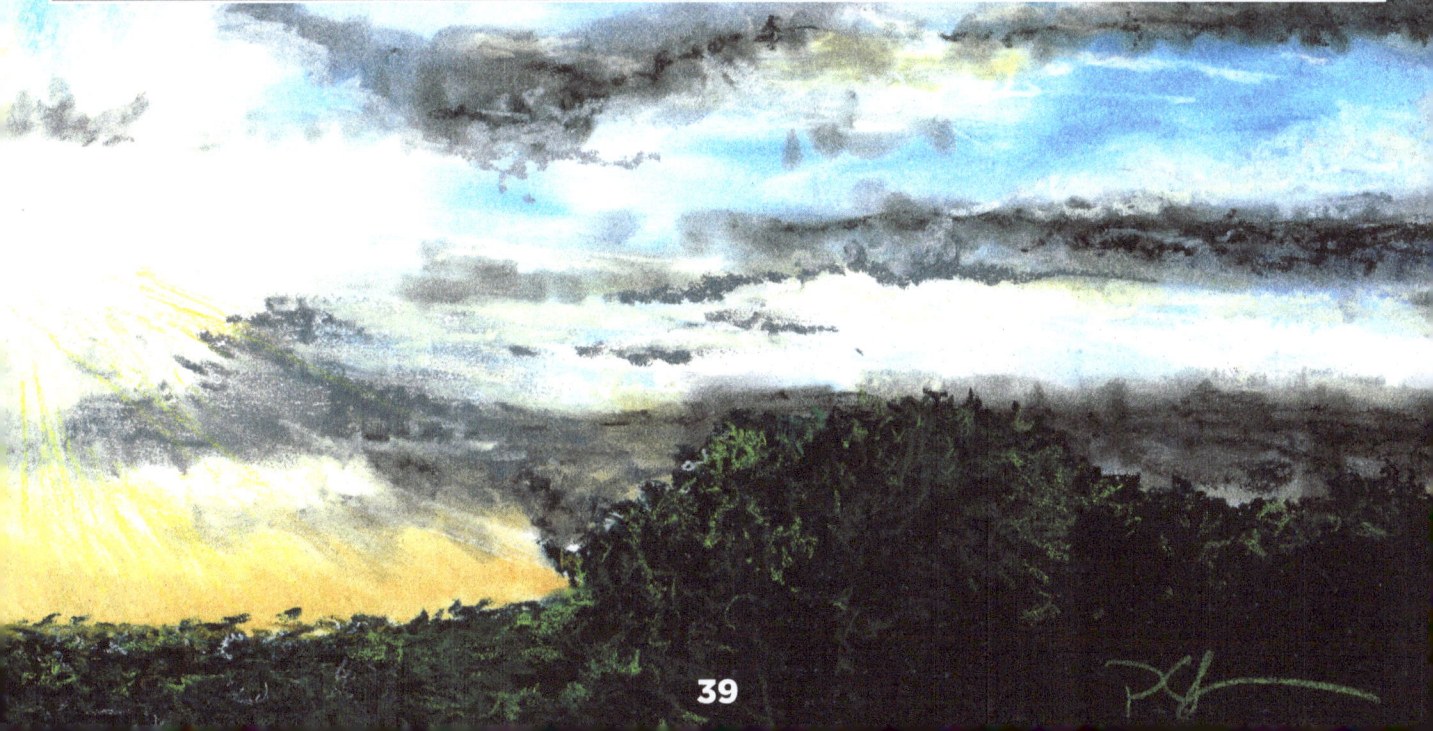

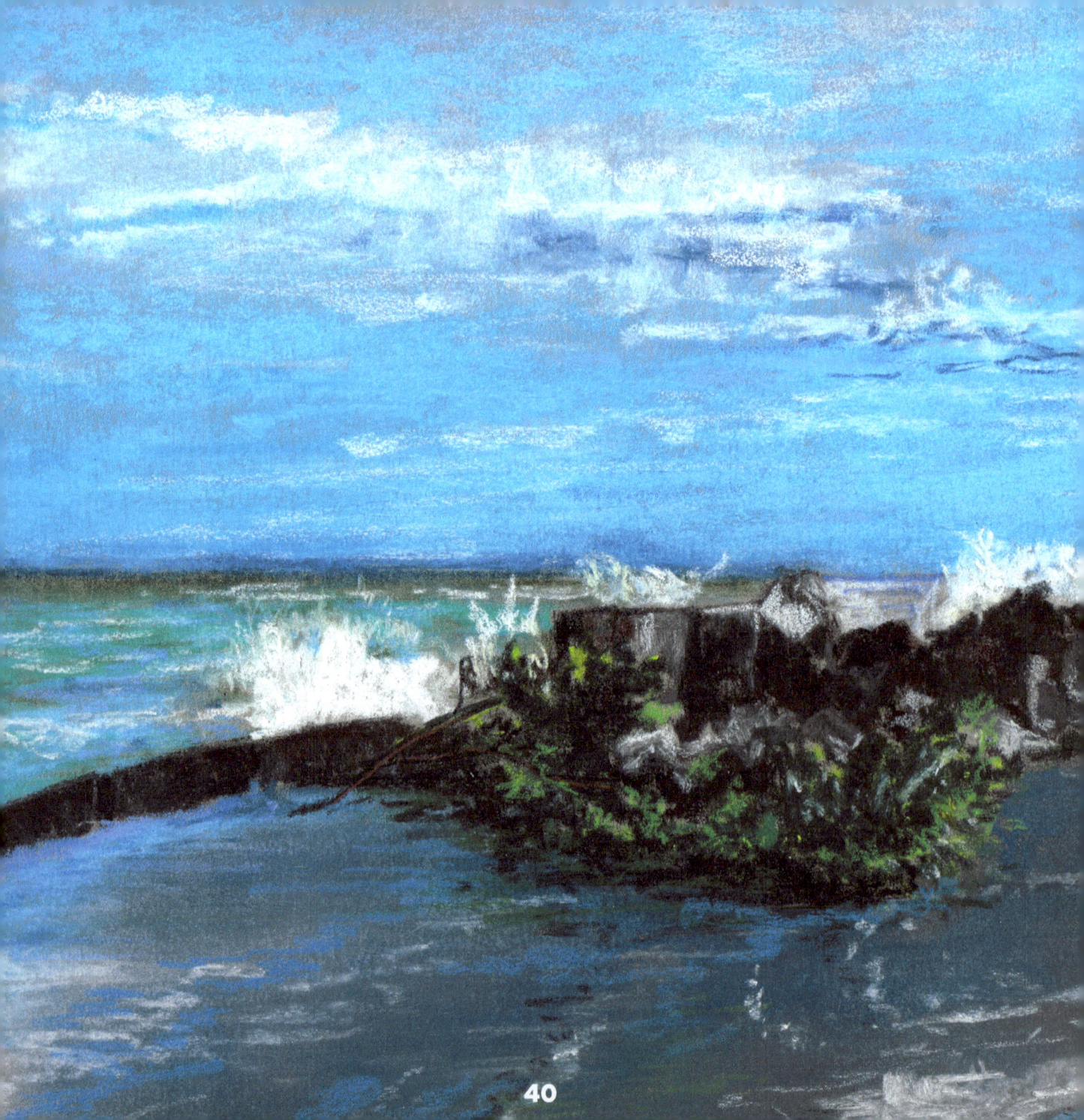

Title: Lake Michigan Breakwall

Size: 15" x 11"

Paper: 400 Grit Sanded Pastel Paper

Insight:
- Pan Pastels and Stick Pastels are used for the background.
- Once I was done with the pastels, I sprayed with a workable fixative, then used the color pencils on top for details and highlights.
- Using pencils on a sanded paper does grind the lead down fast.

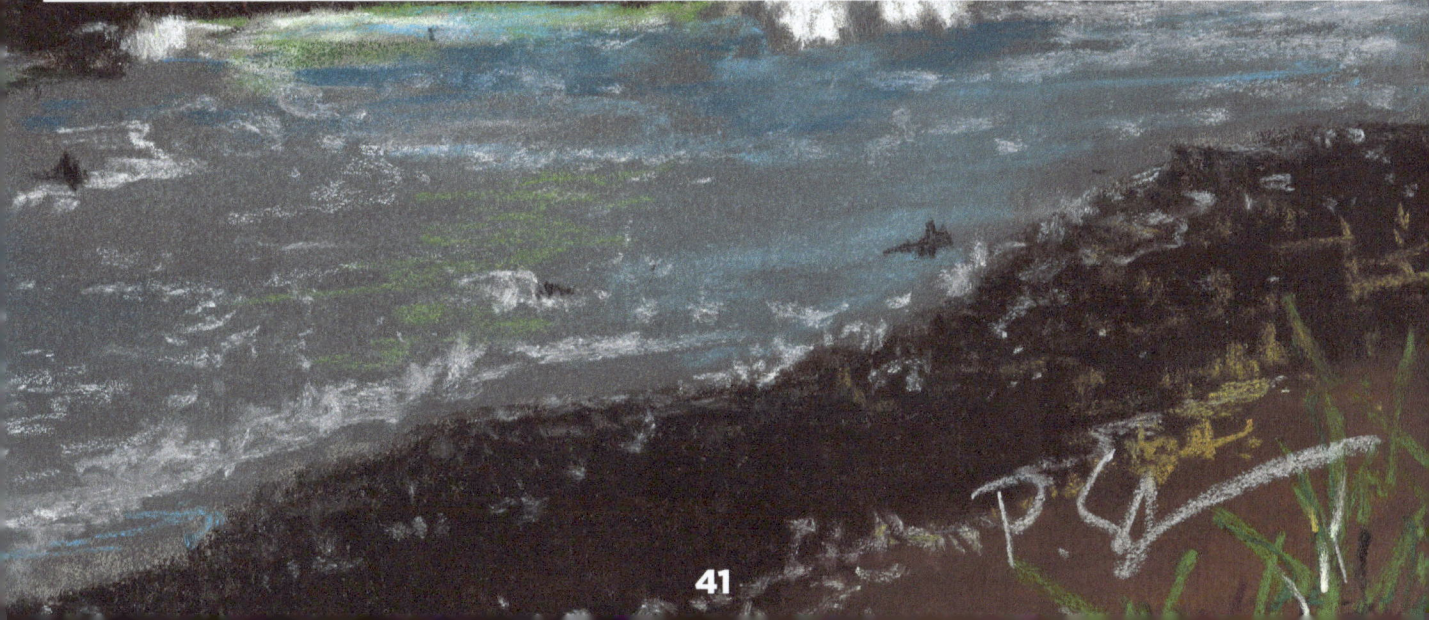

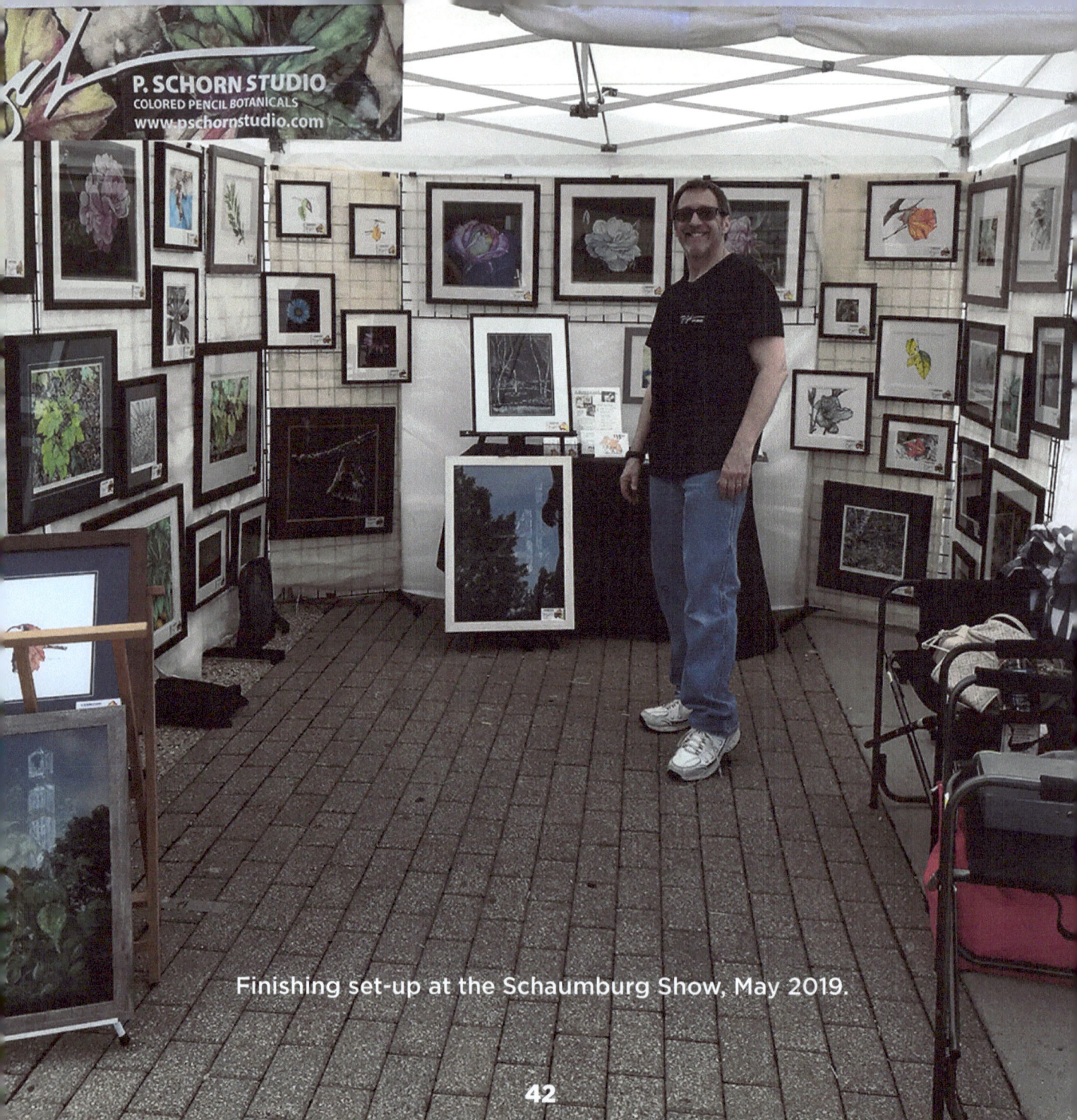

Finishing set-up at the Schaumburg Show, May 2019.

Art Shows

I started doing the outdoor shows in 2017, they are a tremendous amount of work to get ready for. Just having enough art done and framed is costly enough and the cost of the show. It can add up to be an expensive endeavor. To date I have done over a dozen outdoor shows, a newbie compared to many of my fellow artists.

The one thing that I really enjoy about doing the shows is that I get to demonstrate during the course of the day(s). It brings people into my tent and asking a lot of questions. Many are in disbelief that what I'm creating is done with the same color pencil that many of them have been using for years.

I really enjoy talking about my art and how I do it.

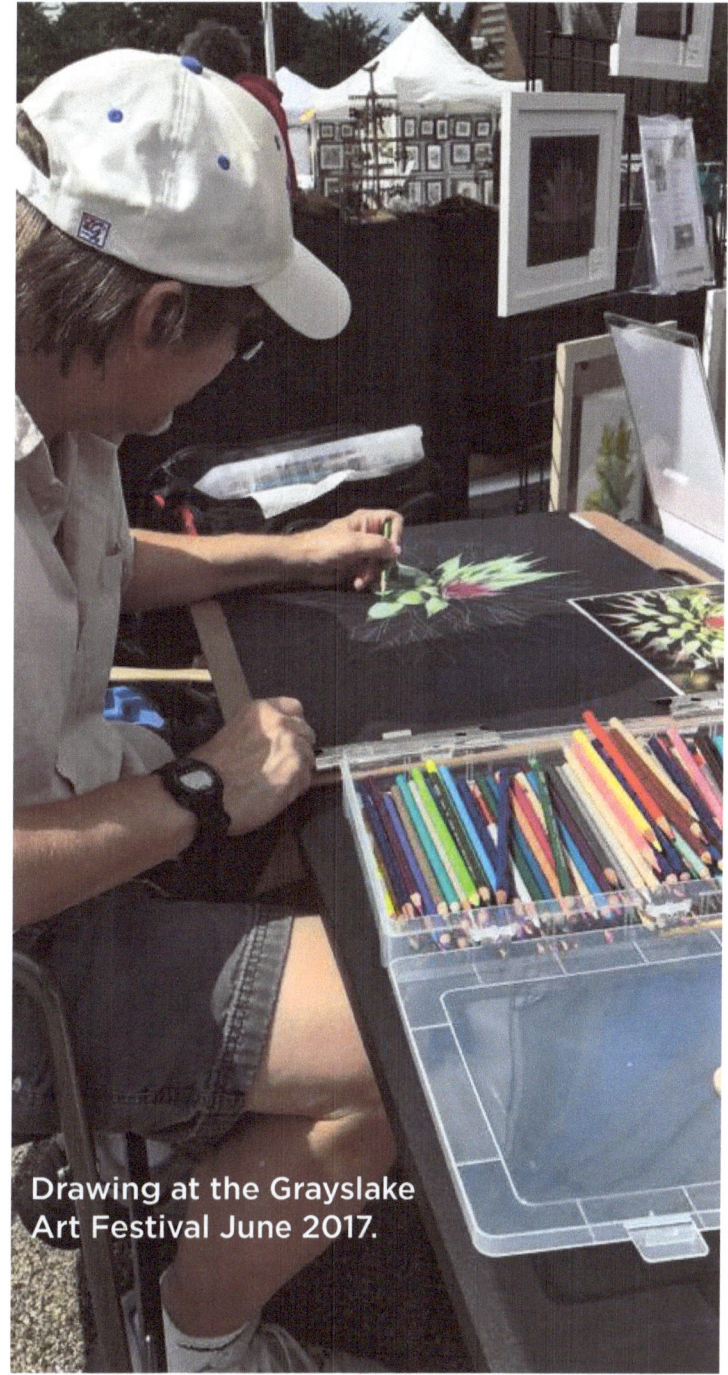

Drawing at the Grayslake Art Festival June 2017.

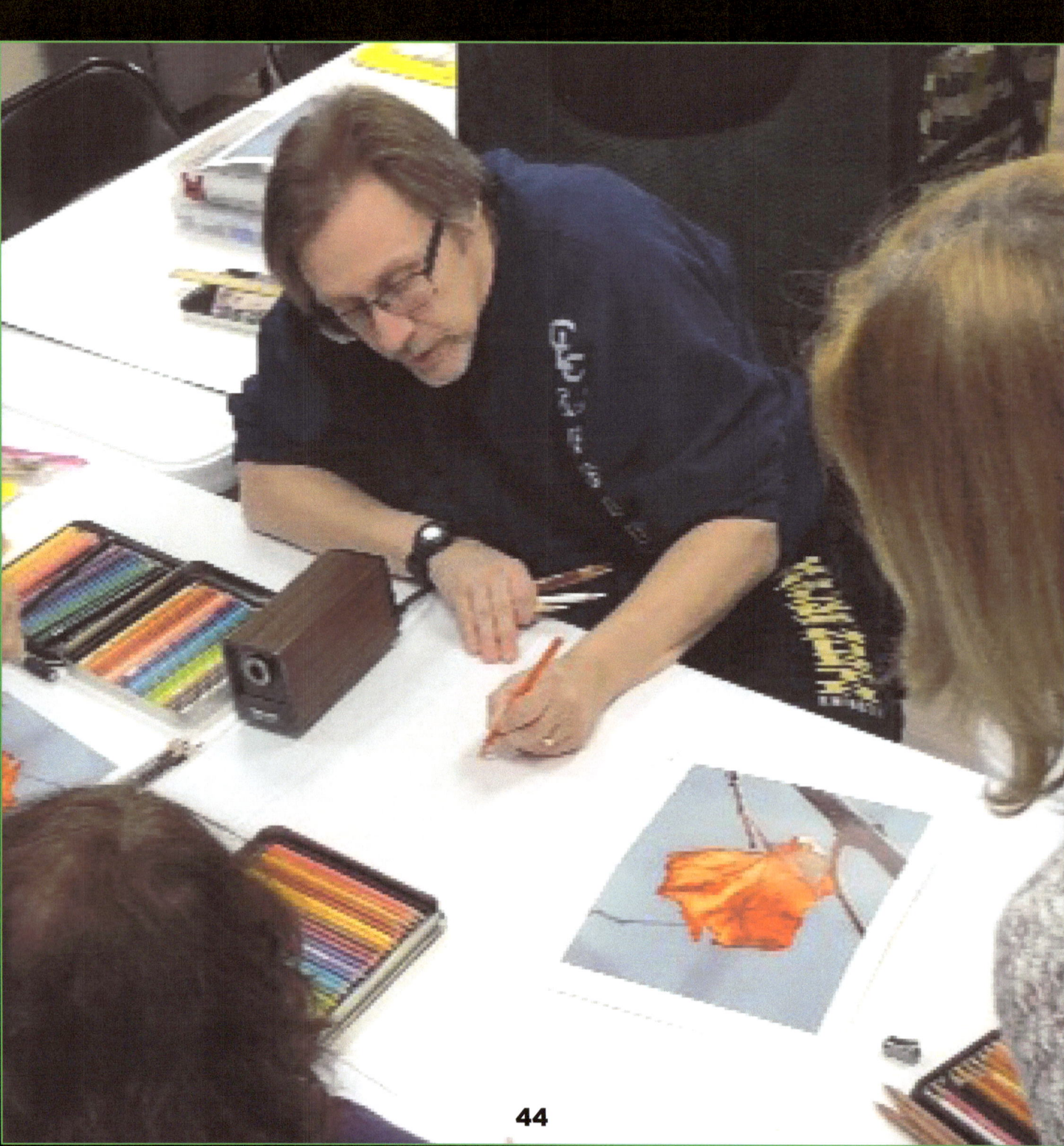

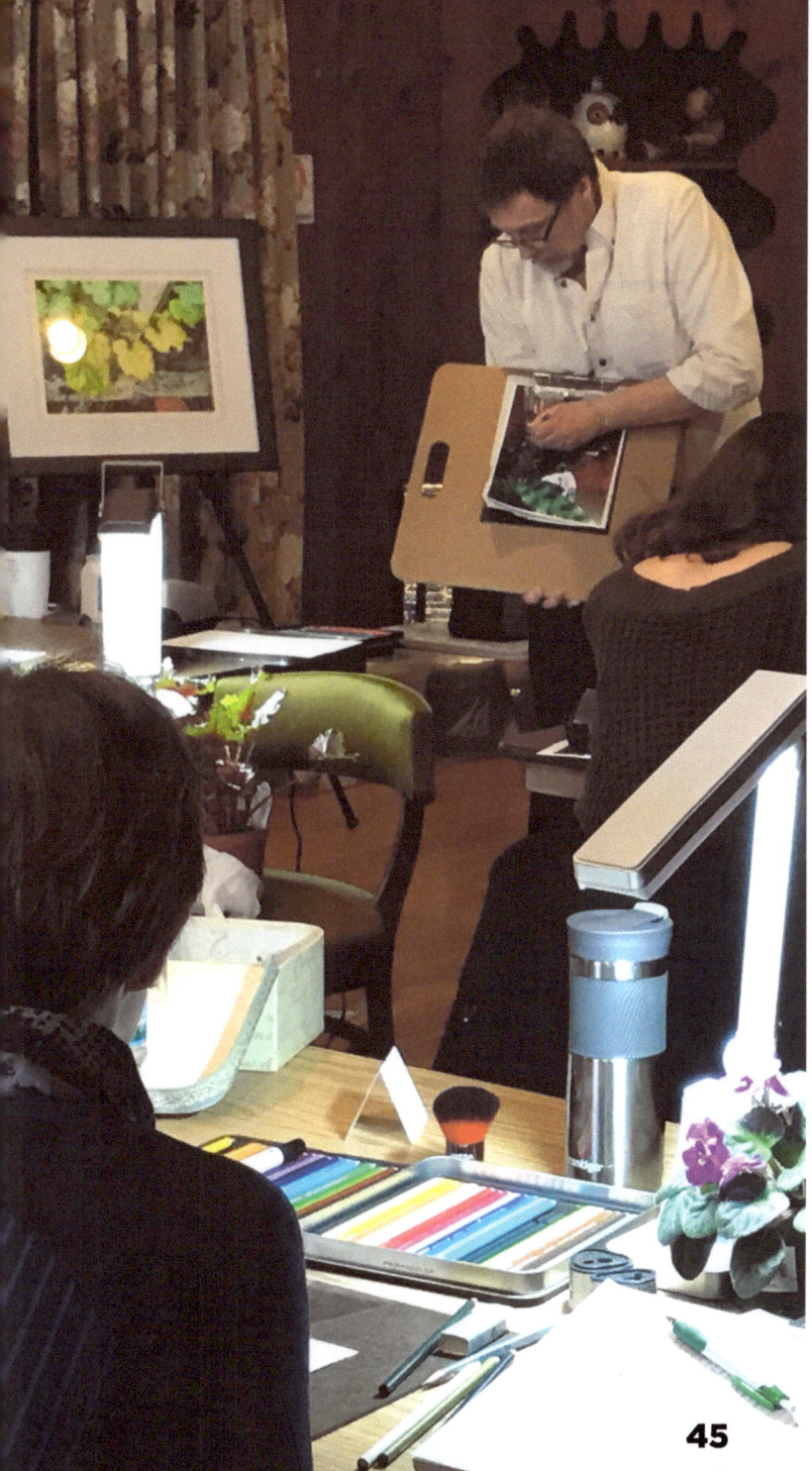

Art Classes and Workshops

I started doing the classes in 2017, a lot of prep to get done for a class. They are tremendously satisfying and fun to do.

I have done approximately two dozen Beginner and Advanced classes combined. I also have had three workshops and a few demos for various art groups over the years.

I find the beginner class a lot of fun, because I get to show them how the "whys" & "hows" to make the pencil look realistic.

Where the more advanced class I usually pick a more specific project and show various techniques along the way. How to get additional detail, under-painting, etc.

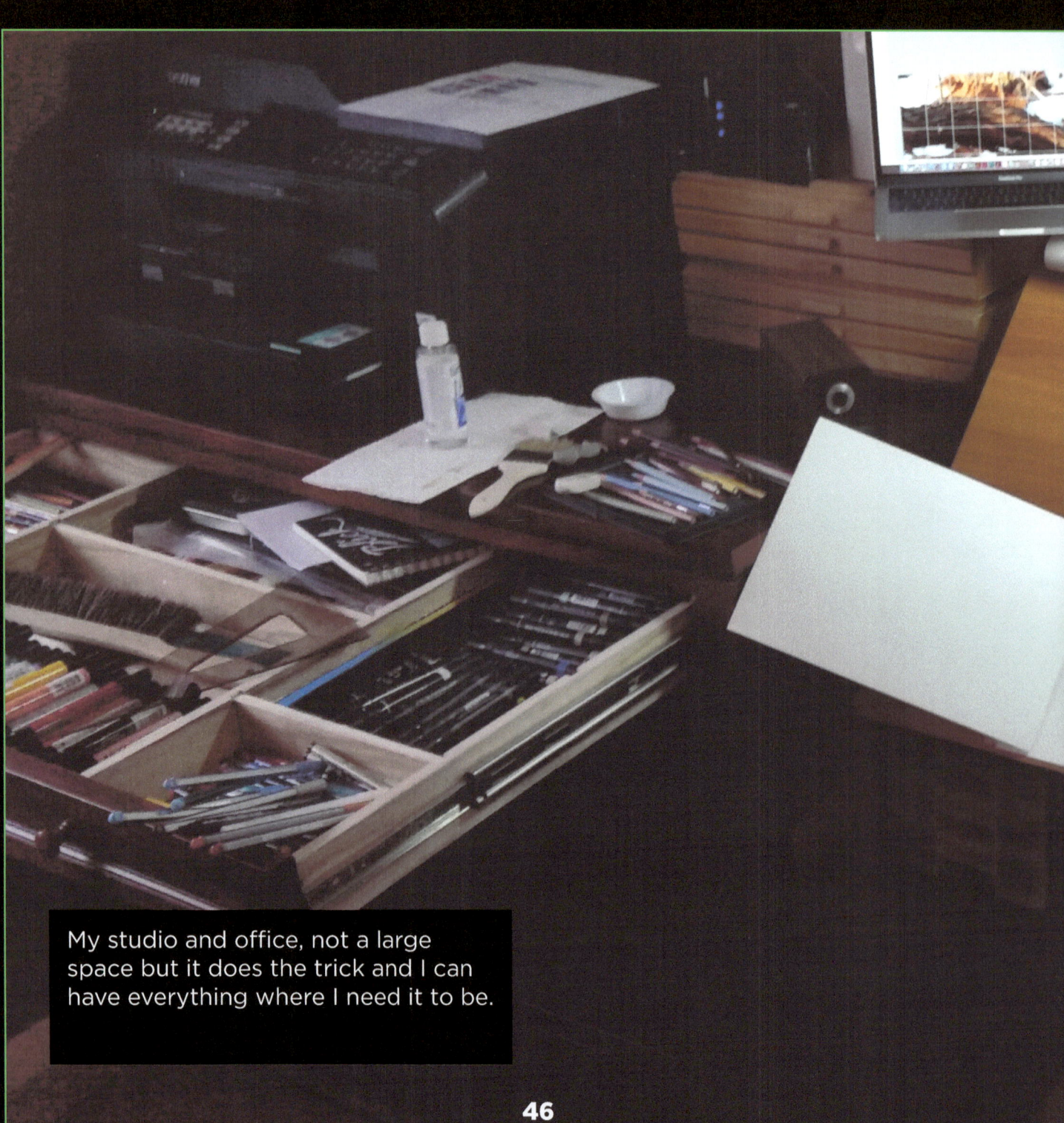

My studio and office, not a large space but it does the trick and I can have everything where I need it to be.

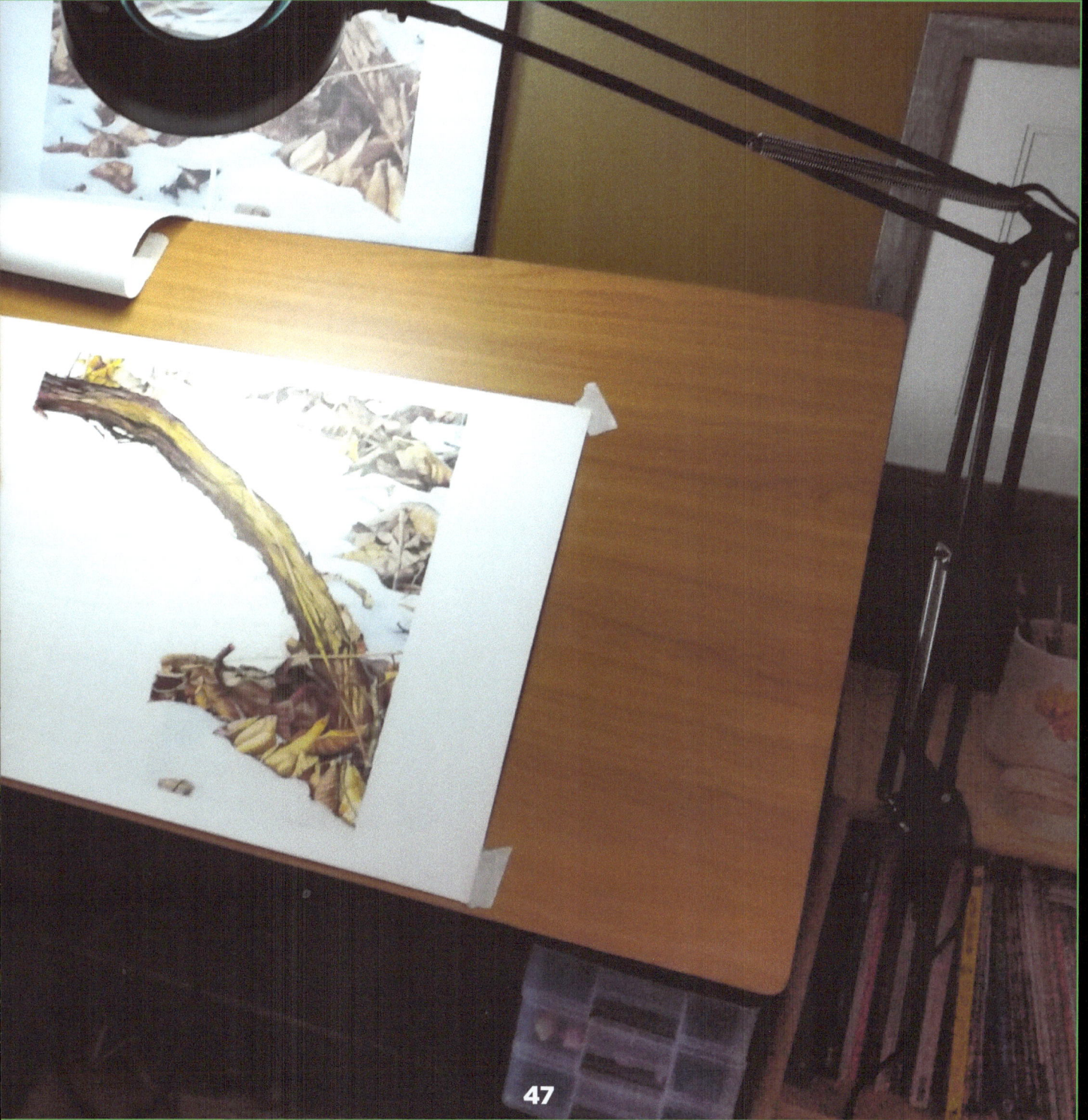

DRAWING TIPS
in no particular order.

TIP - Get the best pencils you can afford, even if it is a few colors, it will make a difference.

TIP - Draw small, keep your strokes no longer than 1/8th of inch.

TIP - All paper has a texture, the better you cover the paper, the more realistic your drawing.

TIP - Keep your pencils sharp. It will help you cover the paper better.

TIP - Draw light and layer your colors. Remember that color pencil is semi-transparent.

TIP - White is an excellent blending color. Remember you mix your colors on the paper.

TIP - Use clear acetate under your hand. It does not smear the colors and you can see through it.

TIP - An ebony pencil is an excellent tool to add details.

TIP - A white gel pen works great to add highlights.

TIP - Do not worry about mistakes, work around them.

TIP - Indigo Blue is an excellent color to darken green.

TIP - A colorless blender pen works great to blend colors.

TIP - When starting a drawing, start on what you think is the hardest part. Only move on when you are satisfied with that portion.

TIP - Use the grid method, it makes what you have to do more manageable.

TIP - When drawing on black paper, remember you cannot erase, it will scuff the paper.

TIP - When drawing from a photograph, remember it is only for reference. Do not let it determine your final result.

TIP - Drawing with color pencil requires patience, IT WILL TAKE TIME.

TIP - Using markers is an excellent way to under-paint parts of your drawing.

TIP - Art Stixs are an excellent way add a different texture to your drawing.

TIP - When finished with your final art, spray it with a final gloss or mat finish. It will enhance the colors and help preserve your work.

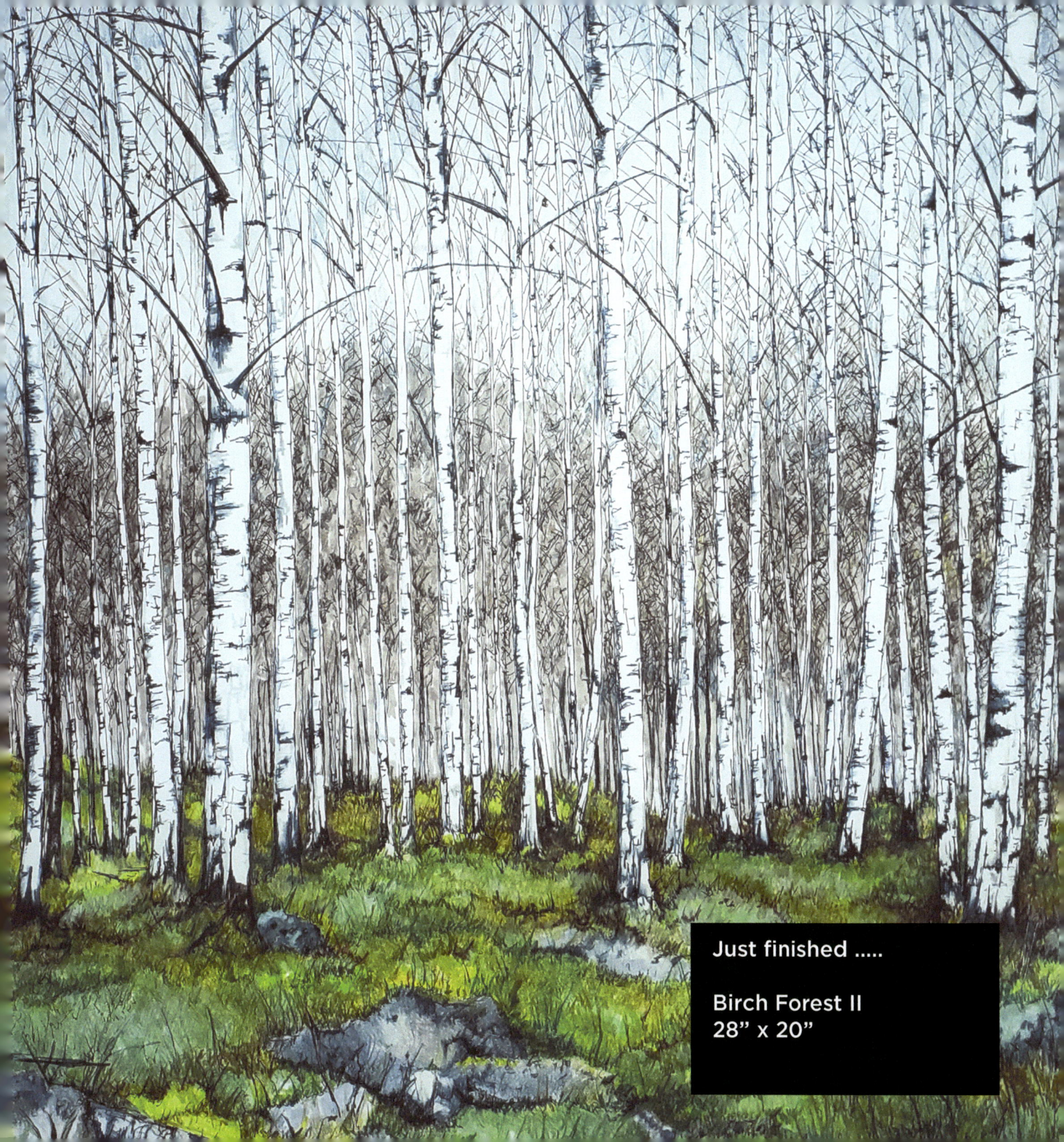

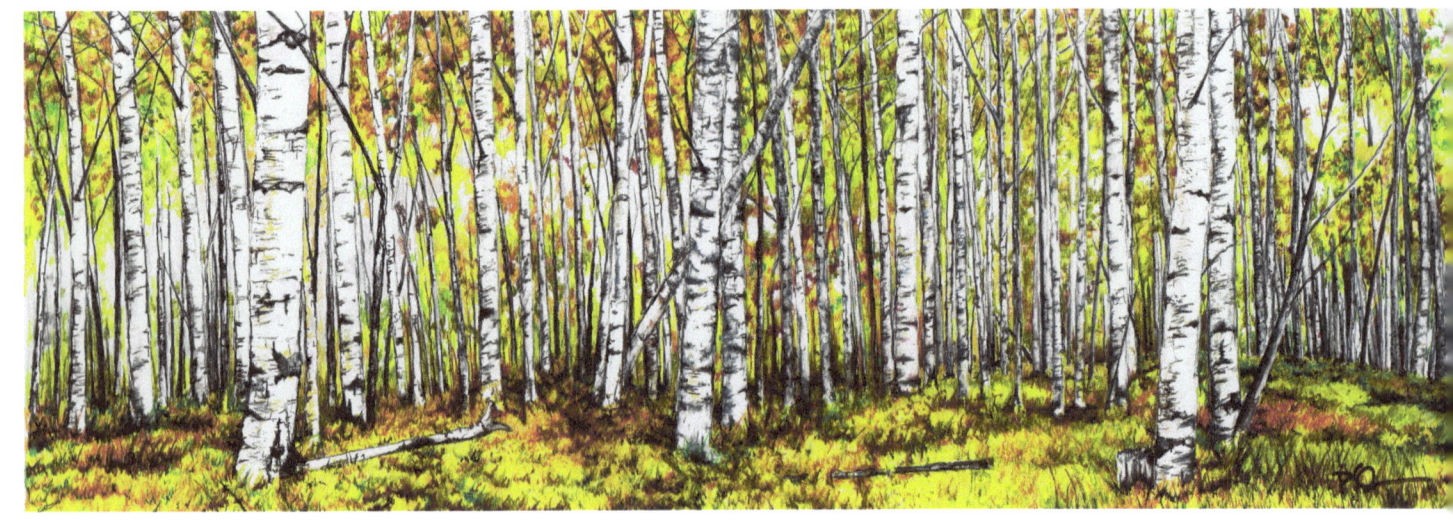

I hope that you enjoy this book as much as I did putting it all together.

If you have questions, comments, tips you want
to share, please send them to me.

phil@pschornstudio.com

pschornstudio.com

A COMPLETE LISTING OF ALL MY ART
CAN BE SEEN AT PSCHORNSTUDIO.COM

All copyrights and reproduction rights are retained by Philip Schorn.
The artwork shown may not be reproduced without the express written consent of Philip Schorn.

www.ingramcontent.com/pod-product-compliance
Lightning Source LLC
Chambersburg PA
CBHW051219220526
45473CB00003B/1091